An American Teacher

Coming of Age, and Coming Out:
The Memoirs of Loretta Coller

Edited by Jon Pahl, Ph.D.

On the Cover: Loretta "Ret" Coller (standing) and Janet "Scarlett" Greene, May 1993

ISBN 978-0-7414-5129-3

Published by:

 PUBLISHING

1094 New DeHaven Street, Suite 100
West Conshohocken, PA 19428-2713
Info@buybooksontheweb.com
www.buybooksontheweb.com
Toll-free (877) BUY BOOK
Local Phone (610) 941-9999
Fax (610) 941-9959

Printed in the United States of America

Published October 2012

CONTENTS

INTRODUCTION

These are the *Memoirs* of the most intriguing person I've known. Loretta Coller was a good friend of my father's. They met in high school, in Shawano, Wisconsin, which is near Green Bay, in 1945. Their friendship endured until Loretta was murdered in Southern California in 1994, in a shocking event I describe in more detail in the Epilogue.

Loretta Coller's life, however, was filled with fascinating twists and turns. She grew up in a working-class Catholic family in Wisconsin, but eventually left the Church, moved to California, and joined the middle class. She was outed as a lesbian by the military during a McCarthy-era inquisition, but then found relative peace and contentment living a "deeply closeted" existence with her life-partner, Dianne Anderson, while teaching high school in a variety of Los Angeles suburban school districts. Near the end of her life, after suffering the loss of Dianne to cancer, Loretta became an activist in lesbian causes and an amateur stand-up comic and disc jockey, while still protecting the privacy of many of her friends and lovers.

I've called Loretta's story *An American Teacher* not only because she was a high school teacher, but because editing her narrative has taught me a great deal. And I suspect her story—when read as a primary-source document about coming-of-age and coming-out in America, will teach any sensitive reader some rather crucial lessons about the shape of American history, and about the need to welcome gays and lesbians into full citizenship in American society.

I first became acquainted with Loretta Coller from passing visits she would make through Wisconsin during my childhood. But I learned to appreciate her humor and hospitality during a 1974 family vacation to California when we stayed for a week at the home Loretta shared in Pomona—a suburb of L.A., with her life-partner Dianne Anderson. Loretta teased the five of us—my family included at the time my father and mother and two younger brothers--that it was the longest week of her life. But she also took us on day tours of the La Brea tar pits, Dodger Stadium, and the Rose Bowl, and she and Dianne and their dogs spent hours with us out by their pool. Loretta was a warm and gracious host. I was fifteen.

I discovered on that visit how funny Loretta was. Her wit made conversation with her a joy—an experience you can have, indirectly, through the pages that follow. On that trip, I also discovered why Loretta was a much loved high school teacher. She was actually able to talk to a teenager like me. Her gifts at communicating also come through clearly in her *Memoirs*. She could craft a well-told tale. What I didn't know in 1974 was that Loretta was a lesbian. My parents never talked with me about Loretta's, or anyone else's, sexual orientation. And at the time Loretta herself was, as she puts it in the manuscript that follows, "deeply closeted." But I perceived very clearly how happy Loretta was with Dianne. I cried when we left.

Since that visit, I've written four books in American history, all of which explore in some way or another the history of American violence. So when I first read Loretta's *Memoirs*, in 2003, I knew that they had to be published. In the light of her murder, they tell a stunning story about the long and tragic consequences of the silencing experienced by so many gays and lesbians in America.[1] From beyond the grave, Loretta Coller's *Memoirs* continue her work as an American teacher. And they're not just for gay and lesbian readers. I think they will be interesting, and enlightening, to almost anyone. One very brief excerpt from her life story has already been published in an anthology of narratives about the experiences of gays and lesbians in the military.[2] With the publication of her entire memoirs, scholars and general readers can now see how this one incident fits within the development of a complete human life.

Six months before her death in 1994, Loretta told me that she'd written her life story. We were sitting on a curb outside her new home in Glendora—a home she'd lived in for five years with the woman who would kill her. Our family was once again depending on Loretta's hospitality. This time we were in California to celebrate the Rose Bowl parade and football game. Wisconsin was playing for the first time since 1963. Loretta simply said, as we sat there watching the sunset, that she'd written her autobiography. She also said she wanted to see it published. By then, I knew she was a lesbian. She had come out to selected friends and acquaintances in 1989. But I didn't know how difficult her coming-of-age had been, so I didn't ask her very good questions at that time. I wasn't much help to her. I suppose she told me because I had published my own first book in 1992. Our conversation about the project was brief, as we shared a southern California sunset together. Six months later Loretta was gone.

After her death, I dimly remembered that Loretta had told me about her *Memoirs*, but I made no effort to track them down. I didn't know where they were, I had no idea whether they were decently written, and I had plenty of other writing projects to occupy my time. It wasn't until late Spring in 2002 that I found out what had happened to the manuscript, after a chance meeting with Loretta's older sister, Bette at the funeral of my uncle, Herb Martin, in Shawano, Wisconsin. Bette had driven up from her home in Menasha. I'd flown in from Philadelphia. My father reintroduced us (we'd met once before), and in a conversation on a window seat in the corner of the funeral home, Bette offered the manuscript to me. I then recalled Loretta's desire to see her life-story in print. I told Bette I'd read whatever she sent me. I made no promises.

It's funny to me, looking back, how fragile all of these connections are. It's surprising to me that I've now spent several years of my life working on this project. When the manuscript finally arrived from Bette, via my father, it was a faint typescript produced by a poor dot-matrix printer, with little or no paragraph structure. It took me another six months to get around to reading it. The book that you're holding hasn't changed drastically from that original. I restructured a few chapters, established consistent paragraph structure, and omitted a few redundancies. The original is now in the archives of the institution where I teach.

My goal in editing was to preserve Loretta Coller's unmistakable voice. I'm pleased, then, that many of her friends who have read the finished work reported afterwards: "I could HEAR her saying that!" For the voice you will hear in the pages to follow is of a distinctive, humane, moving, and funny narrator with subtle insights into living that emerge gradually from her writing—like life's lessons themselves. The story Loretta Coller tells is not sanitized or romanticized. She reveals her mistakes and shortcomings, as well as her successes, in these pages. I can't say the work is likely to become a literary classic. She wasn't a professional writer. Nevertheless, the story she tells is powerful, and affecting. It's changed me. And I suspect it can challenge and change some of the assumptions of almost any reader.

The Memoirs of Loretta Coller fill a niche that historians like me find increasingly fascinating—the lived experience of everyday life as narrated by "ordinary people."[3] Memoirs are usually the privilege of celebrities, or academics. In the case of celebrities, the individual in question might hire a "ghost" writer, who then interviews the celebrity and puts his or her life story into prose. There's a ready market for such books because of the name recognition of the star, so the memoirs get published. Stars sell.[4] These books have their value, but the stories are inevitably written in light of the fame that the stars have achieved. They're biased by the weight of public expectations. They reflect a concern for "posterity."

In the cases of academics, the bias is a little different. Academics like me are used to constructing arguments. That's what we do. Every lecture is an argument, every paper delivered at an academic conference is an argument, and every book is an argument. More or less consciously, we write to promote a cause with which we are personally identified. So when academics write memoirs, as they sometimes do, those memoirs tend to be arguments with an axe-to-grind.[5]

Loretta's *Memoirs* have a clear angle of vision. She has a point to make. But her agenda does not get in the way of the straightforward, amusing, poignant, powerful, and sometimes raw narrative that she weaves. Loretta did not initially write this for "posterity." She wrote to get over her grief, to help her find herself again. She started writing shortly after Dianne died of cancer in 1984. She had no fame to protect. She had no national platform. Only gradually, after finishing the first draft, did she discover that her story might have significance beyond her own purposes. Then, in 1990, she published a brief account of her military years in Mary Ann Humphrey's *My Country, My Right to Serve: Experiences of Gay Men and Women in the Military, World War II to the Present.*

That brief clip reveals that Loretta saw her experiences in at least two contexts—as a coming-of-age story, and as a coming-out story. You don't need this Introduction to understand Loretta's *Memoirs*; the narrative works quite well on its own. But for those who like an interpretive framework to go along with an autobiography, or for those who have an interest in further reading about the historical context of the events Loretta describes, my words can perhaps be helpful.

Loretta's narrative is clearly a coming-out story.[6] The *Memoirs* vividly describe Loretta's early awareness that she had no interest in heterosexual marriage or children, and that she was attracted to the company of women. She does not describe this as a "lesbian" self-awareness, however, until after being outed by the Air Force during a McCarthy-era witch-hunt. Only then does she claim the title "lesbian," ironically embracing her governmentally-imposed identity.[7] Badly hurt by this inquisitorial process, Loretta lived most of the remainder of her life publicly closeted. As she puts it, she was "very homophobic." After being fired from several positions for being honest about her military service, she took to lying on job applications to cover up her sexual orientation. Especially when she turned to teaching as a career, Loretta describes living in daily fear of being exposed as a lesbian—which would, she was convinced, have put her vocation at risk. Even after joining the Southern California Women for Understanding (SCWU)—an organization devoted to education and advocacy on behalf of lesbians, Loretta and her partner Dianne maintained their confidentiality--out of fear.[8]

Loretta's act of writing a memoir, then, was an act of courage that was itself a form of coming-out.[9] By writing, Loretta committed to prose her most vulnerable self. It must have taken some serious consideration on her part to tell me about her venture. I'm grateful that she trusted me. To be sure, by the time she told me about her writing she had ended her career as a teacher, and was increasingly open about her sexuality as a public speaker with the SCWU. But she surely also knew that many lesbians faced fears similar to her own, and who as neither celebrities nor academics had few resources other than their own wits to protect themselves.

I'm confident, in other words, that Loretta Coller sought publication for her *Memoirs* out of a conviction that other lesbians and gay men might benefit from knowing her story. She was willing to risk representing herself in a way that still associated her, in the eyes of many, with shame, in order to strengthen the voices of others who needed to overcome that shame. That her *Memoirs* reveal, in fact, a life of love and compassion, along with more than a measure of joy and contentment, was surely a dimension of being "out" that Loretta hoped to communicate through telling her story.

But I also think Loretta wrote for heterosexual readers, to help those in the sexual majority understand sexual minorities more fully, and to learn to accept them without fear or prejudice. There are, after all, many who still think of homosexuality as a "disease," as "sin," or as something to be frightened by or overcome.[10] There are those who think gays and lesbians should not be teachers.[11] In Loretta's story, as she gently communicates her desires and feelings for other women, it becomes clear that there is nothing in her sexual orientation for anyone to fear. Loretta hoped to live a life of intimacy with another adult she loved. That hope is open to fulfillment for all heterosexuals without question. Why, her *Memoirs* implore us to ask, should she have had to hide who she was? As a "coming-out" narrative, in other words, Loretta's story demystifies a lesbian's life. I believe her story can do much to end stereotypes and misunderstanding.

Loretta's memoirs further suggest that the question of whether homosexuality is genetically-determined or culturally-constructed is a moot point.[12] In lived experience, it doesn't matter if one's desire for a partner of the same sex is "hard-wired" or "soft-wired," a matter of "nature" or "nurture." It simply is. Loretta clearly considered her desire for women a life-long, hard-wired pattern.[13] But the way she described that desire—as "homosexual" or "lesbian," emerges in the narrative only in light of particular historical events or turning points. Similarly, Loretta can describe her desire for women as an "identity," an "orientation," or a "lifestyle." It mattered little to her whether her sexuality was a destiny or a choice. It simply was. It is only when homosexuality is perceived as a "problem," I think she would suggest, that questions about origins become important.[14] Loretta's story reveals, in short, how she crafted a life as a lesbian in which her sexuality was one feature among many in her experience.

Consequently, Loretta's coming-out memoirs also might assist readers to clarify the fear and fascination some harbor about lesbian sexuality. Simply put: sex isn't that significant a part of the story. Some of this may reflect simple modesty on Loretta's part.[15] But shining through her narrative is a much more important strand that situates sexuality within the larger context of the desire for partnership and intimacy. Loretta describes herself as a "hopeless romantic." And while her naïve streak did cause her some problems in life, it hardly qualifies as a disease. Her memoirs reinforce the findings of those historians who suggest that the medical and military establishments together transformed gay and lesbian desire into a hyper-sexualized public panic.[16] Such panic then allowed lesbians to be located somewhere on a continuum of deviance, as historian Lillian Faderman bluntly put it, "between necrophiliacs and those who had sex with chickens."[17] Fortunately, most physicians and psychologists have advanced beyond such prejudicial stereotypes. In a belated if yet significant move, the American Psychological Association removed homosexuality from its list of diseases in 1973. Public opinion in many circles, however, has not yet caught up, and many people—including prominent politicians, continue to stigmatize gay and lesbian desire. Loretta's manuscript clarifies how there might be much to gain for society in affirming gay and lesbian couples, notably by opening marriage to them. When Loretta found her life-partner, she knew that it entailed "a promise of fidelity and a pledge of infinity." By coming out, Loretta came into the mainstream of American society. She claimed her place as a citizen. She was an American teacher.

If Loretta's *Memoirs* constitute a "coming-out" narrative, then, they also tell a "coming-of-age" story that lasted a lifetime. She never stopped learning. As with memoirs generally, coming-of-age stories are often the privilege of the famous or well connected. The genre is venerable in American literature, back at least to Benjamin Franklin's own *Autobiography*, which depicted his life as a gradual ascent through frugality and moral discipline to happiness and success.[18] Fully the first half of Loretta's book describes the process by which she "discovered herself," or established her identity. As is increasingly the case in the U.S., it took her a while, and in many ways her identity remained fluid, in motion, and changing throughout her life.[19] Also, unlike many coming-of-age narratives since Franklin's that celebrate the "self-made" person or independent individual, Loretta describes a maturation that depended on her relationships with others.[20] Her coming-of-age was a coming-into relationship. Unlike the typical male story of individuation, Loretta's maturation came through her discovery of strength through interdependence.[21]

The first few chapters of the memoirs give a vivid depiction of life in a small town for a lesbian child during the poverty of the 1930s. Although the vignettes are brief, they reveal rare insights into the lived experience of a child.[22] Many readers, I suspect, will find entertaining Loretta's stories about her Catholic schooling. She does play on some stereotypes about nuns, but without the bitter spirit often found in what one scholar of Catholicism called the "pissed-off-former-Catholic" genre.[23] Loretta retained little sympathy for the authoritarian structures of the church, but she also writes affectionately about the nuns, and approvingly of the education she received at their hands. "I learned," she simply puts it. Loretta also clearly delighted in the embodied devotionalism that Catholic experience in America evidenced in the 1930s and 40s. She felt so honored to participate in a Marian pageant that she was able to recall it in vivid detail. And she felt chagrined—to the point of tears, at being expelled from the same pageant for breaking another girl's arm in a playground spat. That tale—with its layers of desire just underneath the surface, and imprint of authoritarianism throughout, is a microcosm of the whole of Loretta's life-story. To come-of-age, Loretta Coller had to come-out of the Church.[24] At the same time, she always carried with her the desires, moral sensibilities, and fears that had first been fostered in those Wisconsin schoolrooms.

Loretta describes her high school years as happy, but she does not dwell on them. The absence of any extended narratives about her adolescence disappoints me, as a historian of youth, especially since the few hints she provides about her experience are tantalizing. She generally recalls "being well-liked," and remembers that she danced primarily with other girls at sock-hops and barn dances. Fortunately, I have access to a yearbook from Loretta's graduating class of 1949 at Shawano High School, courtesy of my father, Fred. That yearbook reinforces the perception of a person who was popular and enjoyed a good laugh.

Loretta's senior class photo, for instance, includes the caption underneath: "Bury me in the principal's office, for many's the time I wished I were dead there."

After her graduation, Loretta was a regular at the frequent reunions sponsored by her high school class. It was at her 40th year reunion in 1989 that Loretta came out to her classmates. Few were shocked by the admission, and it did not noticeably change her relationships with any of them. Coming-of-age for Loretta, even at age fifty, was assisted by coming-into relationship with her public school classmates. As she puts it, it had been in high school that her "world opened up." No doubt her choice to become a high school teacher herself was shaped in part by her positive experiences at the public school in Shawano. I share in the Epilogue a few more details about her career as a teacher, and a few of the accolades former students offered to her memory at a service held shortly after her murder.

A significant theme throughout Loretta's coming-of-age story is her varied work experience. Loretta's memoirs are rich with anecdotes about the lived experience of some of these jobs. In her delightful account of a few days she spent on the assembly line in a Wisconsin factory that produced mittens, recorded in Chapter Three, Loretta evokes both the comedy of Lucille Ball and the pathos of sweatshop workers paid by the piece. Loretta grew up in a working class family, and only gradually transitioned into the middle class. She took pride in her work, but was also willing to seek better opportunities for herself. That her work-life also provided her with companions and recreational outlets—softball, basketball, and bowling teams, suggests something important about the history of women's labor.[25] Loretta also narrates in some detail her struggle to keep jobs after being given an undesirable discharge from the Air Force. Her nomadic employment efforts reveal something of the fluidity and transience—yet ready availability, of opportunities for women to work in mid-twentieth-century American economic life.

Like many women in post-war America, Loretta joined the Air Force both for economic opportunity and life experience. She gives a vivid account in Chapter Four of her time in basic training, and then as an Airman at McClellan Air Force Base near Sacramento. She loved the structured life, especially the parades, and the patriotic feelings being in the service evoked in her. Her narrative touches lightly—through Chapters Five and Six, on themes of race and the sadism of military hierarchy. She remembers in particular one officer who ordered her to dig through full garbage cans while on kitchen patrol, in an effort, as she saw it, to humiliate her. She also reveals in vivid detail the intimacy (not necessarily sexual) that women in the military shared in the 1950s. Throughout her narrative, Loretta appears as a hard-working and strong-willed individual who revels in the company of her fellow airmen. Her pride in her country comes through clearly. She is delighted when a promotion to Sergeant is offered to her. And she is shocked when the promotion is rescinded, due to an investigation of her sexual orientation.

Loretta's most detailed account from this time period, in Chapter Six, covers her treatment by the Office of Special Investigations. She describes ruthless and inhumane invasions of her privacy, under pretenses of "security," and describes interrogations riddled with lies and other methods that bordered on torture. Historians have documented well the consequences of McCarthy era anti-Communist paranoia in the cases of celebrities and high-profile individuals. Less well known are the cases of gays and lesbians like Loretta.[26] The one regret that Loretta expresses in her *Memoirs* comes from this period. At a critical point, she was tricked by investigators into outing a lover. It was a betrayal she vowed never to repeat in her life. For Loretta, coming-of-age meant coming into a critical attitude toward her own government.[27] That her well-earned mistrust of authorities would actually prove fatal to her later in life--when she refused to out a lover who eventually killed her-- demonstrates how McCarthy-era repression produced tragic consequences that endured long after the Senator from Wisconsin passed the scene.

But the deepest strand in this coming-of-age narrative is not coming-into mistrust, but growing into a mature, satisfying love. At its core, Loretta's is a love story. After being discharged from the military, Loretta discovered herself among the burgeoning lesbian community in 1950s California, notably at Santa Monica.[28] She describes in Chapters Seven through Nine a free-wheeling, sleep-on-the-beach lifestyle that, following her treatment by the Air Force, suited her. She does not romanticize those years. They included casualties from sexual promiscuity and drug-use. Most vivid among the narratives from these years is Loretta's account of her friend Lynden, who died at age 28 of a heroin overdose, after repeated trips in and out of prison. Lynden's story serves Loretta as a counter-type of her own life-course. She sees in Lynden what she herself might have become, while also telling Lynden's tale to point out the loss of one she felt was a poet. Without making it explicit, Loretta credits her family and schooling for teaching her basic respect, including respect for herself, to avoid the worst excesses and outcomes of the Santa Monica beach scene. Overall, though, the picture of that subculture that emerges from Loretta's narrative is of a loving acceptance that she craved, and failed to find, in the broader culture.

The remaining turning points in Loretta's coming-of-age story all hinge around her loves for Barb, Billie, and Dianne. Loretta treats in just a few pages her relationship with Barb, with whom she lived for two years in Massachusetts after an impulsive and eventful trek across country from California. But she clearly depicts her relationship with Billie in Chapter 10 as the point when her life "took on a whole new meaning." Billie ended Loretta's searching. Billie had found acceptance among her family. That acceptance translated into a person who Loretta described as "stable, dependable, compassionate. . . faithful and steadfast, giving and undemanding." Loretta goes on to recall wondering if it was too late for her to incorporate those attributes into her own personality. Because of Billie, she concludes, "I learned it was not."

For nine years Loretta and Billie lived together. Loretta's life took on the stability that she had sought, and failed to find, in the military. She graduated from college and began her teaching career. The couple bought a house together in Irwindale. And they made friends, notably Lou and Dianne, in the San Fernando Valley. The latter was a teacher, too, and gave Loretta good counsel as she sought her own teaching credentials. As the four women grew closer, an affinity between Loretta and Dianne grew to the point where it blossomed into romantic attraction. Loretta describes in straightforward prose both the growth of that attraction, and the difficult choices it created. She indicates how far she had matured in the way she sought to negotiate the break-up with Billie to begin a life with Dianne. It was a difficult time, and Loretta is honest about the challenges. But those choices also set the stage for the most fulfilling love of Loretta's life.

Part Four of the book—which takes up almost a third of the narrative--describes both the deep satisfaction and devastating loss Loretta experienced in her love for Dianne. Vignettes of their life together, in Chapter 11, depict a domestic tranquility and joy in one another's company that I experienced first hand on my visit with the couple in 1974. The narrative details of how Loretta and Dianne spent their time—playing cards or board games, reading the morning paper over coffee, camping, cooking, voting, studying—demystify their life together, and constitute a poignant ode to joy. When Dianne's melanoma—which she was probably harboring long before it was diagnosed, attacked her aggressively, Loretta unsparingly describes in Chapter 12 the ravages it caused, and the trauma of grief that resulted. All of the facets of losing a love come into play through Loretta's raw prose—denial, shock, bargaining, anger, and pain.

Throughout, like a beacon, is Loretta's steadfast compassion for the one to whom she had promised herself. At times, the narrative is almost painful in its detailed account of embodied suffering. But to touch such raw places in her own emotional memory was undoubtedly essential to the process by which Loretta worked through her grief. In the final pages, then, Loretta offers some modest counsel to others facing loss, based on her own experience. That her chief advice—to talk about the loss, and avoid isolation, meshes well with her own course of healing, found through writing, is no coincidence. Coming-of-age for Loretta Coller meant, finally, owning the gifts of communication that she had been given and that she had cultivated, and then using them to tell her story to others. She was an American teacher.

The Memoirs of Loretta Coller clearly reveal how profoundly she struggled, like many sexual minorities in America, to gain a stable sense of her self. Her struggle was complicated by the way she was treated first by the Church, and then by the State. Through these institutions, Loretta Coller learned to mistrust authority—and to protect her desires and precious relationships in a veil of silence. Her life reveals the subtle ways that abuses of authority can impact a person's life. And her death—which I describe more fully in the Epilogue, reveals how the subtle process of silencing can sometimes explode into violence. An ex-lover murdered Loretta with a gun from her own nightstand. This happened after repeated threats on her life, which Loretta refused to report to the police. Having been disappointed and traumatized by authority, she felt unable to call upon it when she needed it.

Despite the shocking way she died, Loretta Coller's *Memoirs* resist framing as either melodrama or moralizing: She was neither simply a saint or a sinner, nor was she simply a hero or a victim. In her patient and well-crafted narrative, she shares the contours of a life well lived in all of its complexity. Hers was a life marred by disappointment, mistakes, and suffering, to be sure. That it ended in violence, in the context of a culture riddled with guns and rent by other forms of systemic injustice, lends her story a tragic cast.[29] Yet throughout her narrative, Loretta Coller also describes flourishing as a lesbian—and finding fulfillment in some quite ordinary graces. Her ability to describe these ordinary graces makes her life-story rich with wisdom. I know I have learned from this American teacher. I only wish she was still alive today to share in the joys that come from recognizing life's follies, and to laugh with my father and me once more at the warmth of intimate friendship forged despite life's suffering. For it was Loretta Coller's delight in life, and her growing desire to share the wisdom that she had gained, that made her presence fill any room she was in, as her story so vividly and engagingly fills these pages.

TIMELINE OF LORETTA COLLER'S LIFE

Sep. 10, 1931: Born in New London, WI to Irene (d. 1975) and Delbert (d. 1951). Loretta was the youngest of six children.

1938-1943: Attends Most Precious Blood Catholic School, New London

Summer 1943: Family moves 30 miles north to Shawano

1943-45: Attends Sacred Heart Catholic School, Shawano

1945-49: Attends Shawano (Public) High School; active in drama and athletics

1949-51: Employment in Appleton and Twin Cities (Neenah-Menasha), WI at Zwicker Knitting Mills, An Unnamed Slipper Factory, and Kimberly-Clark Corporation

Oct 6, 1951: Begins 8 weeks basic training at Lackland AFB, San Antonio, TX

December, 1951: Training as "Machine Accountant" (computer operator) at Lowry AFB, Denver, CO

March, 1952: Airman Third Class at McClellan AFB, Sacramento, CA

May, 1953: First interrogation regarding "homosexuality" by Office of Special Investigations

July, 1953: Recommended for promotion to Airman First Class (Sergeant); postponed due to ongoing investigation

Sep, 1953: Promised "General Discharge" for "confession" of "homosexuality"

October 1953: Hearing by "Board of Officers"

December 1953: Administratively discharged with "Undesirable" status; escorted off base under military police escort

1954-55: Various employment efforts in Portland, OR; Sacramento, CA; Appleton, WI

June 1955: First residence in Los Angeles; frequents Santa Monica beach community/clubs; works at various jobs

1956-58: Meets Barb—first stable partnership; moves to Westfield, MA

Spring 1958: Breaks up with Barb by mutual agreement; moves to Appleton, WI and takes job with Hardware Mutual Insurance Company

Fall 1958: Transfers to L.A. office; lives in Burbank

Summer 1961: Meets Billie, moves to Ontario, CA; begins college

1967: Graduates from California State, Los Angeles; lies about military service on teaching credential questionnaire; begins career as High School English and Drama teacher

1970: Breaks up with Billie; commits to Dianne

1979: Joins Southern California Women for Understanding as confidential founding member; Loretta petitions USAF for upgrade of discharge status-- granted "Honorable" discharge

1982: Dianne discovers mole that eventually proves cancerous

June 15, 1984: Dianne dies of cancer

1986: First draft of memoirs completed; reworked until 1993

1987: Sells home in Pomona; purchases home in Glendora— invites Janet Greene to move in with her

1990: Publishes brief excerpt of military experiences in Mary Ann Humphrey, *My Country, My Right to Serve*

January 1, 1994: Loretta tells Jon Pahl of memoirs on a visit to her home; recently broke up with Janet Greene

June 18, 1994: Loretta dies of gunshot fired by Janet Greene on the night of June 1, 1994

July 10, 1994: Memorial Service held in Loretta's honor. 150 attend. Service lasts three hours.

THE MEMOIRS OF LORETTA COLLER

Acknowledgments

THANKS – After all these years
To all the women of Flight 1183, 3742nd and WAF Squadron, Lackland AFB;
To the women at McClellan AFB who supported me as best they could;
To the US Government who unknowingly planted the seed of survival that has served me well.

AND THANKS
To the women of SCWU and the San Gabriel Valley who loved and comforted Dianne and who gave so freely of themselves in their support of me; and especially to Irene, Jan, Flo, Coe, Dee, Susen, Dorothy, Jane, Sharon.

AND THANKS
To Juana and Roy for understanding how vulnerable I was as a teacher.

TO

BILLIE, who turned my life around;
DIANNE, who gave me roots and wings;
SCARLETT, who made it okay to love again.

PART ONE:

GROWING UP LESBIAN
IN WISCONSIN, 1931-51

CHAPTER ONE:

CORN MEAL AND GRAPE JELLY

Before I was thirteen I had broken a girl's arm, sworn at a nun, and touched the "Body of Christ." If I had known then that these events were simply an indication of the rest of my life, I still would not have done one thing differently.

Being born during the depression years, 1931 in my case, times were automatically tough. How tough? Consider my sister Irene's reaction upon seeing me for the first time: "Well, she's nice, but there are so many other things we need so much more."

By all financial standards then operative, we were poor. My dad was a house painter and paper-hanger, and in our small town of New London, Wisconsin, jobs were infrequent and money was scarce. I didn't view us as poor, but then I never gave it much thought. My sisters remember the hard times; I do not. Nor do I remember the divisiveness between my mother and dad. There are a few things I vividly remember.

I remember making the weekly trips on Saturday to the Relief Office with my sister Bette. We would pull a small wagon several blocks to the office and the people there would put three or four-pound bags of corn meal and two cans of grape jelly in the wagon and home we'd go. We'd have corn meal balls, corn meal fried, corn meal cooked every way and in everything. We'd have plain grape jelly sandwiches, grape jelly sandwich with peanut butter (this was rare), a tablespoon of grape jelly for a snack, and grape jelly in a cut glass bowl always on the table as a centerpiece.

And to this day, I cannot look at a muffin, a cake, or a bag of corn meal, nor can I face a packet, a jar, or a can of grape jelly.

I remember we moved often. Sometimes we lived in a house, sometimes upstairs over a store or a business. One time we lived in an old hotel that had been converted to small apartments. And one time we lived over a tavern. Our upstairs apartment was directly over the bar. The noise was continuous and loud. Especially on the weekends, the music and the hollering and the dancing would keep me awake until closing time. During the time we lived there my dad was gone a lot. I never knew where he went, but he always brought me something when he came home.

One time it was roller skates. My first pair. My mother was furious. She said it was a foolish waste of money. And where was I going to skate anyway? He also brought her a new set of dishes. I can still see her unpacking them and setting them along the cupboard shelf and on the library table in the dining room. They had a rose pattern and it seemed like there must have been a hundred pieces. As she unpacked the dishes, I put on my new roller skates. I knew I had no place to go, but I just wanted to try them. I got both skates on and stood up. No problem there. I figured I just might be a born champ and would never know unless I tried. I decided to pull myself around the edge of the room by hanging onto the furniture. I was okay until I got to the cupboard area. Then I lost my balance. I tried to grab for the cupboard so I wouldn't fall and hurt myself. My arm and hand went the entire length of the cupboard shelf sending the dishes in every direction. I landed in the middle of the floor surrounded by the remains of my mother's gift. It was three years before I saw those roller skates again.

One of those houses we lived in was just across from the Catholic Church and school. In summer I would go over there and play on the swings and the slides. The nuns were famous for feeding hobos and often when I was there one or two hobos would come to the convent door. The sisters never let them in the convent, but they did invite them into the screened porch. There they set places for them and fed them royally. Although I never went inside the porch, I would talk to the hobos on the other side of the screen. Periodically one would tell me of the places he'd been, of riding the boxcars, and of all the different types of people he'd met. I had no fear of them even though my mother constantly told me not to talk to them. I thought their life fascinating, adventurous, and I envied their independence. Why they were hobos, or how lonesome they were, or how needy they were never entered my mind. To me they were all free souls. And I wished I could be one.

When I was about to enter the seventh grade, we moved to Shawano—about 30 miles North of New London. No one had told me there was a possibility we would move. Usually it didn't bother me, but this time it was with shock I heard my mother say, "Your dad's got a better job in another town and we are moving there." And we did. I hated to leave New London. I didn't have a lot of friends, but the ones I did have I cherished. Then, at what I considered a critical stage in my life, I had to start all over and make new friends.

We moved in the middle of summer. I had five weeks before school started to be all by myself and miserable. And was I ever! I cried a lot at night in bed; I sat on the lawn under a maple tree and cried; I walked down town and cried all the way back. My mother had no patience with my loneliness or my sorrow. "Just wait until school starts" was her solution every day. One day I walked down town, went into the dime store and stole a handful of chocolate covered raisins. Naturally they melted in my hand before I could eat all of them and I was washing the chocolate off my hand at the bubbler when a policeman came up to me and said, "This bubbler is for drinking, young lady. Wait until you get home to wash your hands." It was a rotten time.

Finally the summer ended and school began. Those first two weeks were almost a repetition of the summer. Then one day my dad came home and told us he'd found a house for us. We moved the following weekend and my whole life changed.

The family that lived downstairs in the old house had two kids, a girl named "Tootie" (honest) who was a year older than me and a boy named Bud who was two years older. When they found out I was going to Catholic school, they told me about two girls right in the neighborhood who also went there. Marie lived just around the corner and Phyllis lived about three blocks away. The only awful part was they were both eighth graders—a year ahead of me. But I decided to bite the bullet and face possible rejection. The next day at school I listened as Sister Ruth called roll. I identified them, approached them at recess, and that day we walked home from school together and our friendship began. We remained friends long after graduation from high school. I lost track of Marie a long time ago, but until recently I would still see Phyllis when I would make a trip to Shawano.

When I entered high school, my world opened up. For the first time, I was associating with kids who were not Catholic. There was much pressure not to associate with non-Catholics, not to enter a Protestant church and certainly not to take part in any activities in one. Doing so would forever damn our souls to hell, as any good Catholic knew. I had to walk past two Protestant churches on the way to school every day. As a matter of fact, one was just across the street from the Catholic Church. I was so conscious of the terrible sin of contagion just from walking in front of the Protestant church that I began crossing the street a block before I came upon the church. It was several years before I ever went into a Protestant church and then it was for a wedding. After that, I just knew my soul was impure and my days were numbered.

CHAPTER TWO:

SURVIVING IN A SCHOOL
NAMED FOR BLOOD

I remember my early years in Most Precious Blood Catholic School (I couldn't then, and I can't today, understand why anyone would name a church and a school after ANY kind of blood).

Because I attended a Catholic grade school, the nuns are forever imprinted in my heart, in my mind, and (the nuns were quick to make certain) on my soul. There were two Sisters who made a lasting impression on me. One was Sister Mary Ruth, the one who molded me through the 7th and 8th grades. She belonged to the order of the Sisters of St. Joseph. Every time I see *The Sound of Music* she comes to mind. I can just see her belting out "Climb Every Mountain."

For those years I sat in the front seat. I don't recall any special reason for that arrangement. It seemed to be my destiny to be so close to her that her rosary would bang against my desk as she walked back and forth across the room. I remember wondering if any of those black beads would ever crack or the chain links might break, and wasn't it a sin to bang Jesus against a desk like that?

Often I would put my head down on my desk to sneak a peek up her round white collar. I never saw anything but more white layers of "habit." I suppose it was a natural curiosity on my part. And the stories we would hear about a nun's hair being all shaved off so the veil would lie flat on their heads! This idea led me to stare at the side of her head whenever it was turned at an angle. I knew what a shaved head looked like and for several weeks it seemed my personal mission to get at least one good look at just a small portion of her bare head. Finally one day my persistence paid off and I got my well-deserved peek. It was very disappointing. I saw only a few wisps of hair but it was enough for me to know that nuns do not get their heads shaved.

Sister Ruth smelled of chalk all the time. Even when she was not using the blackboard or carrying a piece of chalk (often using it as an extension of her fingers so her pointing became more threatening), I could distinguish that odor. I remember wondering then if it was possible for someone to use chalk so often that it soaked into her pores and forevermore she would have that smell. Sitting in the front desk I often was so busy watching Jesus swing and inhaling the chalk dust that I missed out on the lessons.

Sister Ruth should have been a pitcher for a major league baseball team. Despite the restrictions of the habit, that woman would pitch an eraser from her position in front of the blackboard at any kid in the room and be deadly accurate. I suppose it came from practice since she did it at least three times a day just to our class. The only times an injustice occurred as a result of the "eraser pitch" was when the target knew it was coming, ducked, and depending upon the angle of the pitch, one of three innocent victims would be clobbered. I was never the designated target but by default I did get eraser scarred twice.

The only other weapon Sister Ruth used frequently and, I might add, effectively, was her 12-inch ruler. As we were doing our assignment, she would walk up and down the aisles between the desks and tap the ruler on each desk as she walked by. I always knew just how close she was to my desk by the increasing sound of the tap. As she tapped, she would glance at the work being done and if it wasn't as it should be, there would be a loud "smack" as the flat of the ruler hit the desk of the unfortunate pupil.

But I learned. I have a solid foundation in the 3 R's that has served me well. Today, thanks to daily mental exercises in arithmetic that Sister Ruth designed, I can do the basics of add, subtract, multiply and divide faster in my head than I can on my calculator.

The other nun whose face I easily recall was Sister St. Anthony. She taught the lower grades and was also the choir nun. My association with her was primarily in the choir. I really liked to sing in church. I loved singing the Mass in Latin, all the Latin hymns, and even the hymns in English. My favorites were the hymns at Benediction, the songs at Christmas and Easter, and other special holidays.

I hated the hymns during Lent. I didn't like Lent at all. It began all wrong for me. First it was going for an early Mass on Ash Wednesday and having the priest put ashes on my forehead – and then wearing them all day since it was a sin to rub them off. The only thing that made that worthwhile was the contest we had to see whose ashes were the darkest, thickest, and would stay on the longest. Besides that, Lent always made a liar out of me. At least that was how I saw it. Since it was expected that I would "give up" something as a penance during those forty days (and nights), by the time the fifth or sixth day of Lent rolled around, I was no longer "giving up" anything and when questioned about it by Sister Ruth, I had to lie or bear the consequences. Even though I was only twelve when Sister Ruth became my conscience, I knew I didn't want to suffer her punishment for not being able to carry out my penance.

Lent was really hard on me. I didn't like the Stations of the Cross. They took so lonnnnnnnggggg. And since I lived across the street from school, it was expected that I would attend more often than those who lived far away. The one thing that made the "Stations" bearable was that the service always ended with Benediction. My fascination with Benediction carried through into my adult life. Many years later when I was into incense burning, I hunted for something that had the same fragrance as Benediction. But I could never duplicate that aroma. I usually settled for something like "Campfire Memories" or "Sentimental Pine".

Sister St. Anthony was a fireball of a choir director. The choir loft was in the rear of the church, and we would always take our designated spots around the organ. It was impossible to change the spot I occupied without her noticing. In addition to being an energetic director, she had an eye and a memory that clicked on automatically when a body wasn't where it should be. But I loved singing in the choir. I should be honest and make it known that the genes that give one the ability to carry a tune are nowhere to be found in any member of my family. I'm not tone deaf; it's just that I can't sing. Couldn't then, can't now. But Sister St. Anthony was a compassionate nun and allowed me to sing in the choir anyway as long as I wasn't loud. For a time I thought I was doing quite well at not being heard until one day she stopped me as we were leaving the church after choir practice.

"Loretta, you cannot sing on the black keys; you cannot sing on the white keys; you sing in the cracks. I am going to have to replace you in the choir."

So much for this compassionate nun! I was really devastated and I hounded her to reconsider. There was no way she could put me back in the choir singing because nuns do not make mistakes. So to shut me up, she gave me the job of passing out the hymnals and writing on the small blackboard in the choir loft the numbers of pages to be sung. I did this gratefully. And Sister St. Anthony was pleased.

Until one Sunday after the Mass had ended and before Benediction began, I collected the hymnals and stacked them on the choir loft railing, a shelf about six inches wide. I had done this before with no problem. This Sunday, however, I had just made two stacks with seven hymnals in each stack and was carrying back the third stack to set on the railing when I lost my balance and fell against the stacks. All but five of the hymnals tumbled over the railing and landed on various parishioners seated below the loft. From then on I was allowed to be in the choir loft under the following conditions: 1) that I did not sing, hum, or in any way participate in the choir activity, 2) that I sat in one of the pews away from the choir, 3) that I never, never approached the railing, 4) that I left the choir loft before the choir, and 5) that I never, never, never asked Sister St. Anthony to let me do anything again that was related to the choir.

Sister St. Anthony was a beautiful woman. At least what I could see of her was beautiful. Her face was beautiful, and when she was directing the choir, her arms and hands would move in a rhythmic motion that was mesmerizing. I remember thinking how pretty she was and wondered what it would feel like for her to hug me. I never had a thought like that about Sister Ruth, but then Sister St. Anthony didn't smell like chalk. She was the only nun I fantasized about and the fantasies always involved being close to her. The other girls in school would have dreams about the new young priest in our parish and when they would discuss him, I retreated into my world with Sister St. Anthony. She was just one of many women who comprised my fantasies in my young years (the ONLY nun, though).

My excommunication from the choir had taken place in 7th grade. It was a year later that I had an encounter with Sister Ruth that today, closing my eyes, I can relive with no effort. The month of May was the month of Mary. We sang (or rather, the choir sang) all the hymns that celebrated Mary, the Mother of God. I loved those hymns. The height of the month was the May Processional held on the last Sunday of the month. This was an elaborate affair, really an extravaganza considering it was done by the eighth grade girls. A statue of Mary was decorated in detail with all the flowers that are available in Wisconsin in May. The statue was then mounted on a wooden platform that had two poles extending from each end (much like the platform Elizabeth Taylor in Cleopatra was transported on). Four girls from the eighth grade were chosen to carry Mary down the aisle in the church for the May Processional. Being chosen was quite an honor. The criteria for determining who was chosen was neither mentioned nor questioned. I do know that part of it was being tall and since I was the tallest girl in the eighth grade (towering over the others by 4-5 inches), my being chosen was almost an accepted fact. Indeed, I was chosen, along with two of my friends and one girl, Sally, I never liked.

Our May processional was no small production, so starting with the last two Saturdays in April rehearsal was in full swing. Beginning with the month of May, we rehearsed two afternoons a week (after school on Wednesday and Friday) and on Saturday morning. I knew this was an important event just because of the number of rehearsals we had. The details were overwhelming: we started down the aisle just as the priest turned from the altar, faced the congregation and closed his book. The pace had to be that of a bride coming down the aisle; the steps were small and the rhythm the same as that of a bride's entrance. Our feet had to be in synch; we looked neither to the left nor to the right as we entered. We came to a complete stop at the end of the aisle and turned simultaneously to face the statue (at which time we counted slowly to ten), shifted our hands on the decorated poles and gently set the platform on the riser that had been decorated especially for this occasion. Then we turned simultaneously to face the altar and after a count of three (silently to ourselves), we slowly turned, walked to the front pew and took our places.

So on the Friday before the last Saturday rehearsal, which was just before the Sunday of the Procession, the four of us Mary-bearers were walking home, discussing the Procession and how wonderful it was that we could be a part of it and how dreadful it was going to be to start high school in the fall. It was all going so perfectly. Then, about a block before we started to split, Sally started in with her taunting verse. I told her to "keep quiet" twice. Then I told her to "shut up." I was really embarrassed and more than a little angry. This fazed her not at all. My next words were "you just better shut up or you'll be sorry." The sing-song verse came again so I grabbed her arm, whirled her around and began pushing up on her wrist. I know that hurts because my brother Jack used to do that to me at home; just to test my pain level, I guess.

Sally was no wimp. I pushed up on her arm, released the pressure, let go and sharply pushed up again. All I wanted her to do was to say she was sorry and that she wouldn't call me "horse collar" again. She started to cry and scream and I figured I'd give it one more good push before I let go. I also wanted her to know I meant business and if I couldn't get her to apologize, at least maybe she'd think twice before she called me names again. So once more I pushed up on her arm and her wrist almost touched the back of her neck. I guess it was at that point that we both heard the same sound: a kind of snap or crack. I let go of Sally's arm, jumped up, and ran towards home.

I stopped a block away from home to catch my breath. Arriving at home breathless would certainly cause either my mom or dad or both to ask questions. So after getting my wind back, I strolled home. I was in the house only long enough to walk to the bathroom when the phone rang. I stopped dead in my tracks in the middle of the bathroom as I heard my dad talking on the phone. It was a surprisingly short conversation. Then my dad, who had raised his voice to me no more than twice in my thirteen years, yelled for me to "get out here." Sally's father had called to tell my dad that I had broken Sally's arm and "for no reason at all." I told my dad what had happened and all he said was "we'll just have to pay the doctor bill." My punishment was in the way he said that and in the way he looked at me. I loved my dad a lot and knowing that I had done something that disappointed him and that, in addition, necessitated an expenditure of money we didn't have, was the severest pain he could have inflicted on me.

At Procession rehearsal the next morning--Saturday, Sally showed up with a cast on her left arm. Naturally all the nuns and the other girls wanted to know what happened. Sally's story made her out to be a victim of an unprovoked attack. In all conscience I just couldn't stand there in that group and let that story go unchallenged. I called her a liar.

14

Before I could let out another word, Sister Ruth clamped her iron hand (the eraser throwing one) around my arm and said, "You come with me, young lady."

The minute I heard "young lady," I knew I was in trouble. She led me down to the end of the hall and stood so close to me I could smell the chalk.

"There is no place in the Procession that honors our Virgin Mary for anyone who argues and fights. You can go home now; we will find someone to replace you."

How could she? I never even got a chance to tell my side of the story. So, both hurt and angry, I looked at Sister Ruth and said, "I didn't want to carry your damn statue anyway," turned and left.

I cried all the way home. Both my mom and dad were there when I walked in. Before they could ask me what was wrong, the phone rang. I had a flash of hatred for Ma Bell. My dad answered the phone and after a conversation just slightly longer than the one the night before, he hung up. He looked at me and asked, "Did you swear at Sister Ruth?" Well, I knew that had been Sister Ruth on the phone and I sure knew better than to say I didn't. That could be calling Sister Ruth a liar. So I owned up to what had happened. My dad just said "okay" and again I felt the same pain.

Two things happened as a result of that incident. The next day I attended the Mass at which the Procession would take place. I stood in the vestibule amidst the crowd of people hoping to go unnoticed. The statue came in carried by my two friends, by Sally (wearing her cast like a badge of honor), and the fourth girl who had taken my place. My disappointment at not being involved was instantly replaced by glee. The fourth girl's feet were not in synch and she was a good three inches shorter than the shortest girl. Consequently, Mary listed at a very strange angle as she was carried down the aisle. How sweet it was!

I had long known I was attracted to girls although I didn't put any sexual connotation to it. Nor did I have a name for it. I just knew these things: I liked being with girls; I was not attracted to boys; children and marriage never figured in my plans for the future. And walking home that day, it occurred to me that Sally was a lot like me. And maybe the reason I didn't like her was because she was cuter than I and because Sister St. Anthony hugged her.

I think one of the reasons I'm so disillusioned, disappointed, and disgusted with Catholicism is that I feel I was lied to. There were so many areas of sin that if violated surely meant a black mark on my soul. And if this black mark was not erased by a "good" confession, I was certainly damned. I grew up going to parochial school during the 30's when it was a sin to eat meat on Friday, a sin to eat or drink after midnight if I intended to receive communion in the morning, a sin to miss Mass on Sunday (unless on my death bed and then a priest would come to me so it wouldn't be a sin), a sin to touch the Eucharist once it was placed in your mouth, a sin to tell or think dirty jokes, a sin to be disrespectful to a nun (I just knew my whole soul was the color of midnight as a result of the May Procession incident). I was a total believer and, consequently, I knew that seldom was my soul pure. I was deathly afraid to go to sleep at night without making a "good" act of contrition. The pictures that the idea of hell conjured up in my very vivid imagination became real when I would awake in the middle of the night and realize I had fallen asleep without saying my "Act."

I resent having to go without water all those hours, all those years so I could receive communion in the morning when, now, parishioners can walk down the aisle on their way to communion drinking iced tea if they want to. Sometimes, not often, I would secretly and silently challenge God's law. I remember one Sunday after receiving communion I was walking back to my pew in the choir loft (far removed from the choir members). Not unlike other communicants, I was shifting the "host" or "wafer" around in my mouth with my tongue. This was not easy because my mouth usually was very dry by the time I received communion (since I hadn't had anything to eat or drink since midnight), and since the host itself was bone dry. But one Sunday I merely wanted to shift it in my mouth, hoping to

16

activate my saliva glands. I pressed the flat of my tongue against my bottom teeth and just sort of scraped the wafer along the top end of my teeth. The host fell in the space between my bottom teeth and my lower lip.

I felt panic, fearing that the wafer might just slide out between my lips. God! Wouldn't that be awful? I knew that would get me a one-way ticket no matter how many "good" confessions I made or "good acts" I said. I maneuvered the host back into my mouth and in the process it somehow got stuck on the roof of my mouth way toward the back. I was climbing the steps to the choir loft and I knew if my face was scrunched up when Sister St. Anthony saw me, there would be no penance too big. I pressed my tongue against the edge of the host to try to pry it loose. It was almost as though it was stuck there by suction. So I tried the same trick from the front edge of the wafer. No go. By this time I was nearing the top step into the choir loft. I had a decision to make. Should I risk eternal damnation into hell by committing a sin and touching the wafer thus freeing it from the roof of my mouth or should I try to tolerate the bizarre sensation that the wafer was causing and not make an effort to loosen it?

I made my decision. I stuck my forefinger into my mouth and loosened the wafer. Then I waited to be struck dead (or at least for my finger to fall off). I figured that even though touching the host was a sin, what better way to die than just after communion and in church? Besides, my innocent mind reminded me, if I was made in God's image and likeness, then he must have had something stuck in the roof of his mouth at some time, too, and he would understand, being the understanding God he was. I thanked God for understanding and promised never to touch the host again. And I never did.

I was always confused by some of the ways of the church. For instance, there were indulgences I could say 50 times and for whomever I said them would get so many years knocked off their time in purgatory. There was no point in saying these indulgences for people who had gone to hell, but those in purgatory could benefit from them. Even though I never asked about it, I often wondered who kept track of all the souls in purgatory and how long they had to be there and how much time was taken off by those who said indulgences for them. Seemed like a lot of bookwork for somebody.

In addition to indulgences, I could say ejaculations. (Now, there's a word for you!) These ejaculations, like indulgences, if said enough times could lighten the sentence of someone in purgatory. Of course, we all like to think that those we loved went to heaven, but if by some chance they did end up in purgatory, it was consoling to know we could help them by saying either of these two. The neat thing about both indulgences and ejaculations was that they usually consisted of just one sentence and I could say them any place, any time. And it counted. There was always the off chance, of course, that the loved one went to hell; in which case, all the indulgences and ejaculations were for naught. It was all very confusing because I never knew 1) if the loved one was in purgatory to begin with, 2) how much time the loved one had to spend there so I knew when to stop helping him/her, 3) if there were others helping the same person and I was way on the credit side for someone who was released already.

Of course, novenas did the same thing except they were much more complicated in that they took longer and if I didn't complete them, they didn't count. For example, there was one novena that took five Fridays to complete. If I said four (and they had to be consecutive Fridays) and didn't make the fifth one, the first four didn't count. I always thought that was really unfair of God. It seemed to me if I completed four of the five Fridays, I should get 4/5 of the total applied to whomever I wanted who was in Purgatory. But that was not to be. I stayed pretty much away from novenas.

The Fridays of my parochial school years will forever remain in my mind as days of fish and pancakes. My mother was not an imaginative cook and so she did not fix creative meals. To this day I do not even like to catch fish, let alone eat them and unless the pancake is disguised by some nationality (Swedish pancakes, German pancakes), I'll pass, thanks.

We were taught in the beginning grades never to question. What the nuns and priests told us, we believed. It didn't matter whether it dealt only with Catholicism or with the world in general. We did not differentiate. Everything was accepted and believed solely on blind faith. This lesson stayed with me into my adult years and carried over into my every day living. I did not question authority. Whenever anyone I envisioned as an authority figure told me something, I accepted it as a fact. It never occurred to me that I had not only the right to question, but a responsibility to myself to question. Recognition of this was a long time coming.

CHAPTER THREE:

HOW I LEARNED SANITARY PADS
MAKE GOOD PACKING MATERIAL

Even though there was little money in our family, I never felt I was denied anything. I wasn't expected to work during my high school years and except for a few weeks during the summer between my junior and senior years, I didn't. I knew that after graduating from high school I would go some place into the work force. That was about as specific as my thoughts were. In school I was an average student. I didn't study hard; I only studied enough to be certain I would not fail. I had a good time. My high school years still make me smile. I was involved and well liked. About the only events I didn't participate in were the social ones like the prom and the homecoming dances, where it was necessary to have a date and wear a formal gown. I knew dating was the last thing I needed, or wanted, and me in a formal was akin to a guy in drag.

At any rate, I made no particular preparations for my future during my high school years. I knew that I wouldn't go to college; no one in our family had. I think if anyone had gone, it should have been my sister Irene. She was so successful in her career with the telephone company without a college education, I can only imagine to what levels she would have risen with one. But it was not to be. There was no money, for one thing, and for another we were not an education-oriented family. And as for me, I had had enough school.

Wasting no time after graduation, I went to the Unemployment Office, filled out the necessary form, took a typing test and had an oral interview with the placement lady.

"No office work at this time," she told me. However, if I really wanted to work, there was an opening at Zwicker Knitting Mills in Appleton. I said without hesitation, "I'll take it."

It wasn't that simple. Because of the nature of the job, I had to take a dexterity test. I had heard about these tests, but never believed they really existed. I was put in a small room alone, until a man came in and placed a 12" x 12" board in front of me. It was filled with holes of different sizes and shapes. Next to the board he placed a box of pegs. I couldn't believe it! He was going to ask me to put those pegs in those holes. I was really insulted. I was also broke. So, need took precedence over pride. He told me I had 90 seconds to get all the pegs in the right holes. I remember how angry I got as he demonstrated how certain pegs fit into only certain holes. And I thought, "I must really look stupid." I now knew that a "square peg in a round hole" was not only an expression. After he satisfied himself that I understood what I was supposed to do, he gave me the "go ahead" signal. I figure there must have been at least 64 holes across and 64 holes up and down. Mentally I did a fast tally on the basis of 50 x 50. Was he kidding? He wanted me to plug in over 2500 crazily shaped holes? I mean these holes had shapes I have not seen since. But I bit the bullet and began. I managed to get 11 pegs safely home before he said "stop".

He released me to the original woman who looked at my test results, looked at me, looked at the test results again, then looked back at me and spoke in a "that's all right you little nitwit" kind of tone.

"I'm sure the job at Zwicker's factory would not involve anything as intricate, so I'm going to send you over there for an interview." Happy Day!

I drove to Zwicker's Knitting Mills, parked my car and jaunted into the office. I was pretty sure I could get this job. I didn't even know what the job was except I knew there was no way under the heavens a knitting mill would need someone to play with pegs. The interview went well; I was hired. The personnel woman called for the foreman who appeared almost instantly. This seemed like a real fast-moving day. He walked me out into the factory, over to where the mitten stretching and shaping was being done as piecework.

We stopped by a woman who stood in front of one of the many stretching and shaping devices. There must have been 15 of these machines, all in a row and each with one woman working with it. I had never seen anything like it. Coming out from under a hot covered area on a conveyer belt were frames of hands—one hand after another-- shaped by metal. There was the hand and then the thumb. These little hand frames came past the woman about one every two seconds. On her left was a mountain of mittens. Not in pairs or any kind of separation, just a mountain of mittens. As these frames came past, she would whip a mitten from the mountain, place it on the frame, straighten it so the seam would be directly on the frame all around the mitten, push down on the area between where the index finger and thumb would be in the mitten, give it a final smoothing on both sides and go to the next frame.

That was only half the job. As the frame with the mitten on it went into the covered area, it was steamed into shape. Then, still on the same conveyor belt, it would come out of the covered area and pass in front of her. It was then her job to remove the mitten from the frame, stack it on top of the other shaped mittens in a box on the floor and quickly whip another mitten onto the frame. I was in awe. First I couldn't believe that anyone could do that; second, I couldn't believe that anyone WOULD do that. As I looked past the woman in front of me, I saw four other women all doing the same thing at practically the same rate.

The foreman said, "Over here, Loretta." I followed him to the "Station" next to the woman I had been watching. The machine was not in motion. All those little mitten frames were just sitting there reaching out to me, or at least that's how I saw it. The foreman pushed the on button and the mitten frames responded. The big covered area in the back went into high gear with a loud "hiss." There was already a mountain of mittens for me to work from, and a huge empty box on the floor waiting to be filled.

"You saw the process, Loretta," he said. "Just do the same thing Alice was doing and you'll get the hang of it real quick. You're on your own; ring for me if you have any problems Alice can't help you with." Any problems Alice can't help me with? How about asking her to help me find another job?

Nevertheless, I picked up the first mitten and waited until I was sure I could whip it on a frame. I made several false starts as the frames kept passing by me. The entire unit of frames must have made five trips around when Alice chimed in.

"Just give it a try. You'll get the hang of it real fast. It took me a while before I could hit every frame. Don't worry, honey."

Not wanting to disappoint her, I leaned forward to catch a frame as it first appeared. I stretched as far as I could and slipped a mitten over the frame. Damn! It was only down half way. I followed the frame around in front of me, all the while waiting to get the mitten all the way down and even around the top and thumb. I followed it right up until it disappeared into the steamer. The rest of the frames passed in front of me, all empty. I decided to wait until my mitten came back to me before I attempted to fit another frame.

It wasn't long before my mitten made its appearance from the steamer. Oh, God! The top of the thumb was hanging half off and the seam was about where my knuckles would be if I were wearing it. I pulled it off the frame. What should I do with this?

Alice looked over at me and said, "Send it through again. Just remember to press out the crease that's been made at the top where the seam should be." Press out the crease? She had to be kidding. I could barely get the mitten on half way and now she wants me to smooth it out? I pulled at the mitten, tried to stretch the thumb and waited until the right frame came along. I leaned forward and put the mitten on the first frame out of the steamer, hurriedly straightened it and before I could get the thumb seam on the frame evenly, the frame disappeared into the steamer. Well, I would just wait again.

Alice glanced over at me as all the empty frames went by and said, "You really should try to get more than one mitten on at a time. You'll never master it the way you are doing it." I knew she was right. I didn't want to lose this job. They just weren't that easy to find. By the time I had decided to put another mitten on the frame, my precious one came out. It looked great if I hadn't glanced at the thumb.

"How many times can you send the same mitten through?" I asked. Alice shrugged, "Depends. It should really only go through one time. This is the shaping and stretching of the mitten and you can't shape and stretch it too many times before it loses its elasticity and then we can't sell it."

On the basis of my first two tries, I decided it would be impossible for me to get the mitten AND the thumb on right at the same time. If either of these weren't right again, the mitten would be tossed and it would come out of my salary.

"I suppose a screwed-up third try is too many."

"Yeh," said Alice. "But it might not be a bad idea to keep using that mitten until you get the rhythm going. That one will be rejected now and there's no point in you ruining more and having to pay for them."

I could certainly follow that thinking! I sent my mitten through four more times. The last time I felt like I had "gotten the rhythm." I tossed the severely creased mitten with its permanently bent thumb into the box marked "Rejects." I grabbed another mitten and waited for a frame. I had the whole process outlined in my mind. I would get that mitten on exactly as it should be and when it reappeared I would remove it and put on another one. I'd do that three times and then I'd cover two frames for a couple of turns and gradually work my way up to full coverage of all the frames.

By the time the buzzer rang, signaling day's end, I had reached only a point of success with two frames. Alice assured me that by the end of the following day I would be "on top of it." I walked the two blocks home and when my mother asked me how my first day on the job was, I just looked at her.

The next morning at 7:00 AM I was on the job, ready to take charge and earn some money. As piecework, my salary depended upon my output. I got paid by how many "pieces" I turned out at the end of the day. I remember the interviewer telling me that each mitten pressed was worth one cent and if I really worked, I could earn good money. With the bonus given, some women were earning over $15 a day. I knew Alice was one of these women. I suspected she was part robot.

But, I turned on my machine, psyched myself up, picked up a mitten and attacked the first frame that came by. I missed, of course, and the rest of the morning was pretty much a repeat. By noon, I had filled one box of twelve dozen and had five mittens lying on the bottom of the next box.

When four o'clock rolled around and the buzzer proclaimed the end of the day, I had stretched and pressed another 2/3 of a box. Not bad for my first full day, I thought.

At 3:15 my second day, the foreman came by, tapped me on the shoulder and motioned for me to follow him. We went into the same room where I had first come in contact with him. He shut the door.

"Sit down, Loretta," he said. "Well, how do you like your job?" I thought of all the things I could say in answer to that--none of them acceptable in public. I thought of words I could say that would be non-committal, but acceptable. Words like "interesting" and "challenging." Finally I said, "It's different."

He looked at me as though he'd never heard that word before. "You know, Loretta, usually we can tell after one day whether a person is going to be able to do this job or not. There's a certain knack involved, a skill, if you will. I know it takes some getting used to, but those who are able to master it can normally do it in one day. Their output indicates their ability to do the kind of job we need done. I noticed by the count here (he picked up a graph sheet) that you average about 31 mittens an hour. You should be able to do at least 50 an hour your first day. Alice averages 210 an hour. Of course, she's been here about 17 years."

Seventeen years? My God! My mind reeled at the thought of the number of times that mitten frame had gone around in front of her.

"So, Loretta, after a conference with the personnel manager, we've come to the conclusion you do not have the dexterity for this job. Unfortunately, we'll have to let you go." He handed me an envelope, which I knew contained my paycheck. "I'm really sorry it didn't work out."

I took the envelope, gave him a weak smile and left. I wouldn't even get a chance to say goodbye to Alice. When I was a block away from the knitting mill, I opened the envelope. Counting my first day of training, I had put in just about 20 hours. My check totaled $3.32.

There wasn't much I liked about that job. I didn't like applying for it. And I didn't like getting fired. And now I had to face my mother. Even though she rarely asked questions, I knew it didn't stop her from thinking them. Now what? Back to the unemployment office, I guess. Surely I would encounter the same woman who had sent me to Zwicker's and she would ask for an explanation. That's okay; there have to be lots of people who can't hit a mitten frame square on with a mitten.

I had little motivation left in me the next morning as I climbed the steps to the unemployment office. I knew I had to have a job, but how many times in this small town can I get fired before it becomes common knowledge?

I walked into the office and there sat the same woman I had seen just three days ago. She motioned me to sit. I started to explain why I was here again and before I got a chance, she said, "Mr. Noonan from Zwicker's called me yesterday. Well, some jobs just don't work out. Let's see what else we have here." She went through her stack of cards.

"Do you have any PBX experience?" "No."

"Do you take shorthand?" "No."

"Too bad. Here's a good job but you have to take dictation. Have you had any bookkeeping training?" "No."

"Well, here's one. It's another factory job. Are you interested?" Oh, sure. You bet. I'd really like to get myself into another factory job. Wonderful. "What kind of a job is it?" I asked.

"It's for a slipper company. They make bedroom slippers, mostly for little kids. Most of the slippers have an animal's head in the instep. They insert a squeaker into the instep of the slipper and then when the child walks the slipper makes a noise appropriate of that animal."

Dear God! "And what would my job be?" I asked.

"Well, the slippers would come to you complete as a slipper. There is just one step after yours. The slipper would come to you with the side of the animal not sewn up. It would be your job to insert into the underside of the animal the appropriate squeaker. Then from you it would go to the stitcher who would sew the animal to the slipper. Then, of course, to inspection, packaging and shipping. What do you think?"

What do I think? You don't want to know what I think. "I'll give it a try," I said with a smile.

"Fine," she smiled back. "Go there tomorrow. It's too late today. And let me know how it turns out." I took the referral card and left.

The next morning I was ready once again to meet the world head on. This time the world squeaks. I checked the referral card and saw that where the name and address of the company should be, there was only a blank. Aha! The interviewer at the employment office had screwed up! Okay, so no one's perfect. Looking through the telephone directory, I found the number of the unemployment office, dialed it and waited. Soon a voice answered. I wasn't sure what to say.

"Yesterday, I was interviewed by a lady at your office for a job. I don't remember the lady's name and the company I'm supposed to go to isn't written on the referral card. Can you help me?"

"You say you were interviewed here yesterday?"

"Yes."

"What is your name please?" I gave it to her. Pause.

"I don't have a record here of interviewing anyone by that name."

"Probably not," I said. "I don't think you are the woman I talked to. But can you check your cards and tell me the address and name of the company where I'm supposed to go?"

"What kind of a job was this?" she asked.

I will admit I felt a little strange telling her. "It has something to do with putting squeaks in shoes." The minute I said it I knew I had made a terrible mistake. Long, long pause.

Then, in a voice so sympathetic and consoling, I heard, "Oh, dear child, someone's playing a joke on you. A cruel joke. No one puts squeaks in shoes." And she hung up.

It took me several minutes to get my thoughts together. What had I done wrong? I looked again in the phone book only to discover that the area had two employment offices. I copied down the number of the office I had not called and began dialing again. My mind was really bouncing off the walls.

She was right, of course. I imagine shoe manufacturers spend countless millions making sure shoes don't squeak.

This time the voice answering the phone sounded familiar. I identified myself and spelled out the problem. She apologetically gave me the name and address of the company and the name of the woman I was to see.

For this job, I had to drive about four miles. The address had a half number on it so I knew it wouldn't be a big factory. Maybe that was in my favor. I spotted the number, parked the car, climbed the stairs, approached the first desk I came to, identified myself and my mission to the trying-hard-to-be-natural-blonde sitting behind it, and asked to speak to Lorraine. The blonde kicked her chair into half a twirl and yelled, "Lorraine" out into the open second floor. There were no individual rooms, no partitions, no offices, just an open second floor filled with countless cardboard boxes, fabrics of all colors and textures, four machines that I suspected were sewing machines of some kind, a small coffee area, and about half a dozen tables. Lorraine answered the call with an "Okay" and a moment later I saw a woman get up from behind one of the tables and come toward me.

I again identified myself and showed her the referral card. She was pleased to see me since they were short handed and with Christmas approaching, they were already getting behind in their orders.

"Did they tell you what you were going to be doing?"

I felt silly but I said, "Yeh, something about putting squeaks in shoes."

"That's partly true," she said, as she began to walk back into the cavern. I guessed I was supposed to follow her. "We manufacture little kids bedroom slippers," she continued, "and we put animal heads on them. Some slippers will squeak when the kid walks, others will only oink or growl or whinny or do whatever that particular animal does."

She smiled. I smiled. Funny, I thought, I've seen these things in the stores but it never dawned on me that someone somewhere had to make them. And for now, that someone apparently was me.

As she led me to a table at the back of the cavern, the other four women raised their heads only long enough to see what was happening. I hoped that wasn't an indication of their friendliness, but rather reflected the pressure of finishing all of the orders Lorraine had talked about. We stopped at a table surrounded by open boxes. Lorraine started identifying them:

"These larger boxes contain the slippers; each box, of course, has only one kind of animal slipper in it. There are the dogs, the cows, horses, etc. In these smaller boxes are the sound units."

I looked at those. The boxes were clearly labeled: Bark, Tweet, Whinny, Moo, Quack, Grrrrr, Meeoow, and Ooinnk. A very logical series of thoughts pranced through my mind. Here I was, 18 years old, a relatively intelligent person with a congenial personality, a social attitude, a good sense of humor, and sound of body. What in the hell was I doing here talking to this woman about Quacks and Tweets? This was followed by another logical thought that made more sense: I needed a job.

Lorraine had moved around behind the table, shoved some boxes out of the way to make standing room, picked up a slipper and began to demonstrate the technique of putting squeaks in shoes. I knew from the onset that this was one job I could master in no time. A simple matter of slipping the "sound unit" under the animal until it was in there snugly and dropping it into a box. When the box was filled, I took it to Joyce "over there" who would squeeze it to be certain the sound matched the animal and then stitch the animal to the slipper.

"Are you ready to start?" Lorraine smiled again. "Yeah."

She picked up one of the larger boxes and dumped the contents onto the table. Shades of the mountains of mittens! Now looking back at me was a pile of pigs. Lorraine leaned down and picked up the box marked "Ooinnk." She set the box on the table, said, "It's all yours!" and left.

I managed to finish that box of pigs plus one more of ducks and a box of cows by noon. Lorraine was pleased. We were behind on the orders for "Whinneys" and "Grrrrrs." That's how they referred to them. Never by the animal name, but by the sound they made. My vocabulary suffered while I was at the job. I mastered this technique rather speedily except for the "Tweets." The bird was considerably smaller than the rest of the animals, yet the sound unit was the same size as the rest. In addition, it was easier to identify the front and back of the other units than it was for the "Tweet."

Consequently, two things happened. First, it took me longer to insert the Tweet, and second, I finished one box and was heavily into the second when Mae (the stitcher) brought back the full box.

"I thinks these Tweets are all in backwards," she said. "No sound comes out and I'm sure the units are good. Will you check them?"

Of course, there's nothing I'd rather do than check 200 Tweets and, chances are, take them out, turn them around, and re-insert them. What I said was, "Sure." She was right and I had to re-do all of them.

This was not a bad job, as factory jobs go. I stayed three weeks and then one morning driving to work I knew that if I spent another day with those squeaks, I'd be making funny sounds. I told Lorraine that day that I would finish out the week but that was it. She understood and was really great about it, even offering me a couple pairs of slippers. I declined knowing that I didn't need a slipper to remember that job. In a way, I hated leaving. The women were all accepting of me, never asked any questions, and from the onset included me in their coffee breaks and lunches.

It's strange how some apparently insignificant things stay with me almost as long as significant ones. To this day whenever I hear someone's shoe squeak as they walk, I have a moment of trauma and my eyes immediately go to their feet.

My sister Bette had been working as a statistical typist in Neenah at Kimberly Clark Corporation, well-known manufacturers of Kleenex, Kotex, and a number of other paper products. When she decided to quit and have a baby, she recommended me for her job. Paper manufacturing is one of the mainstays in the area and if it was possible for me to find employment with one of the paper mills, I would be practically guaranteed a job (a good one) for life. Kimberly Clark Corp. is, of course, one of the biggest. So I jumped at the chance. I interviewed and was hired.

Statistical typing is not a bundle of fun and that's all I did. I typed manufacturing reports, loading and unloading reports, comparative production statistics, percentage of waste analyses, and financial statements. I typed columns of figures representing sales of sanitary napkins over the last five years; columns of production figures; columns of chemical analysis of our various paper products; columns of figures whose titles I never even understood. It was a boring, tiring job. But it paid well.

There were the regular fringe benefits that accompany any job, but with this one came a unique fringe benefit: all the sanitary napkins I wanted. In all the women's restrooms was a huge box filled with them and they were mine for the taking. No one ever asked how many I took or in any way did they expect them to be accounted for. I knew this was something I was going to need for the next couple of decades. So each day I would take a dozen or so home. I was just "padding" my future, so to speak.

Seven months after I started building my stockpile, I had a hysterectomy. The doctor had discovered some problems with my ovaries so even though I was only nineteen, the appropriate procedure seemed to be surgery. It was okay with me since I had no desire to have children. But then I had a chilling thought. What does one do with 1680 sanitary napkins? It took a while, but I eventually discovered the following: some can be used for dust cloths; they make great shoulder pads; the outer piece of cheesecloth can be tied to the end of the hose from the washing machine and acts as a lint trap; twenty-eight of them can be sewn together in two layers of fourteen covered with a wild print material and used as a seat cushion. Finally, since they are so flexible, they are very useful as packing material when shipping anything fragile.

Boring and tiring though the job may have been, I liked working at KC. I joined the bowling team, had several crushes on several women, received the appropriate accolades for a job well done, and enjoyed good rapport with my boss. I was well-liked and I knew it. So, a year and a half later when I felt a need to make a change, it was not due to my unhappiness with my job.

But I did not want to fall into the trap of staying at home so long that it became impossible for me to move. Nor did I want to get to the point where I felt I couldn't change jobs because of time and money invested. Another thing, and perhaps the most important, was that I wanted to be in an area where I could be my own person. I knew I was ready to be with people who saw life from the same perspective I did, and I also wanted to see some other parts of the nation. I wanted to travel a little.

As I was growing up, we never had a car so trips to Shawano Lake, or to Milwaukee or Green Bay belonged to somebody else. If we couldn't get there by walking, we didn't go. The ideas of living my life as I saw fit to live it and living it in a place I could choose came together at the same time.

One of the solutions common at the time was to join some branch of the service. And so it came to pass that one day I paused in front of the Armed Forces Recruiting Office. A few days later, I went in. I made a total of three visits to the recruiting officer. I listened as he told me about the travel and education opportunities, the free medical/dental care, good pay, job security, retirement options, the px bargains, 30 days vacation a year, and advancement possibilities. After the third visit, I made up my mind. In retrospect, I did a rather remarkable thing for a sheltered twenty-year-old. I had weighed all this information, considered the military and civilian possibilities, and made the decision to enlist. I knew this was a turning point in my life and I wanted to be successful so I incorporated in my decision to enlist the determination to make the Air Force my career. I knew I was going to like military life; I was going to be successful there; I was going to make it my life –anything else never entered my mind.

When I told my mother about my plans, she didn't understand. She did not say I shouldn't do it. She just didn't understand why I would want to leave a perfectly good job, my friends, and her to go some place strange where I didn't know anyone or have any idea of what would happen. I couldn't explain it to her; I couldn't explain it to myself. I just knew it was time to move on.

One thing I did know was that I loved a parade. And maybe that was an added attraction the service held for me. I mean, I REALLY LOVED A PARADE! Anytime I had a chance to march in one, which wasn't often, I did, and every time I had a chance to see a parade, I was one of the first at curbside. In my fantasy I could see myself in the Air Force blue uniform, looking extremely handsome (I believe a woman can look handsome) and proudly marching down Main Street, USA. But that attraction was secondary to the opportunities the recruiting sergeant had outlined for me. In late September 1951, I was sworn into the United States Air Force and left immediately on the train for Texas to begin eight weeks of basic training.

PART TWO:

BETRAYED BY MILITARY SERVICE, 1951-53

CHAPTER FOUR:

BASIC TRAINING
WITH CORPORAL "TATER"

October 6, 1951 is a day I remember like yesterday. The blue bus (Air Force blue, I later learned) turned left off the highway and headed for an arch that read THE GATEWAY TO THE AIR FORCE across the top. Hanging from the arch was a wooden plaque identifying this gateway as the entry to Lackland AFB, San Antonio, Texas. Further down were two additional pieces of information: CENTER OF BASIC AIRMAN INDOCTRINATION and HOME OF THE USAF OFFICER CANDIDATE SCHOOL.

My heart raced. I was in the company of eight other women and thirty-one men I did not know. It was October in Texas. That meant dust and heat. I had no honest idea of what lay ahead. But it didn't matter. I was committed. I was ready. I was about to launch my Air Force career. True, my enlistment was for only four years, but I had already decided I was not only going to love this life, but was going to devote myself to it.

The bus stopped at the entrance to the WAF area. Two large signs on either side of the road proclaimed "OFF LIMITS TO MALE PERSONNEL." After a nod from the Air Police housed in the little shed a few feet beyond the signs, the bus moved again down an asphalt road. We rode past a large open area where groups of women wearing khaki brown dresses, pith helmets, and boots were marching in formation in all directions. I could hear the calls, "Left, Left,

Left" and my mind boggled trying to take it all in. A row of barracks appeared and the bus halted in front of the one numbered 1354. The door hissed open and the driver shouted, "All women out here." I unstuck myself from the hot seat, picked up my suitcase, and followed the first three women.

As I stepped down from the bus, I must have been some picture. The back of my dress was wet from leaning against that hot seat and the light blue material of my dress had turned dark blue under my arms. My underwear had done an admirable job of absorbing most of the sweat in that area causing it to stick to my body. I cannot fail to mention my garter belt. It was new and stiff. The garters were chafing against my legs in two places: immediately above the stocking line and immediately below the elastic strap. My nylons were glued to my legs with perspiration; my ankles were so swollen from sitting that the skin flopped over my shoes.

Waiting for us was a WAF Corporal dressed in a tan Khaki skirt with two sharp creases down the front, buttoned at the neck, and finished off with a khaki tie neatly tucked into the shirt between the second and third buttons. She wore military issue hose, brown stub heeled pumps, and a khaki flight cap sitting squarely on her head. This was Corporal Tater. I know, I know. I had to suppress a chuckle when she introduced herself. I may have come from a small town, but I didn't just fall off the turnip truck and I had seen enough movies to know that one does NOT laugh at the Tactical Instructor's name upon arrival at basic training. I did find out later that her two co-flight instructors called her "Spud."

She led the nine of us into 1354 and stopped just inside the door.

"This is Barracks 1354," she said. "Remember that number because from now on this is your home. All the barracks look alike so you'd better not forget where you live." Then she called everyone into the hall. She did this with a simple "1354, Front and Center."

I thought it was a miracle. How did she manage to get together all these women so quickly? In fact, until a "flight" was formed (and it took at least 45 women to form a flight), no one was allowed out of the barracks area. This way the women could be summoned with a whisper and at a moment's notice.

When we were all in the hallway, Corporal Tater spoke: "With the arrival of these nine women, we now number 48. Consequently, Flight 183 is now in existence. Tomorrow morning you begin eight weeks of basic training. Lights out at nine o'clock. Muster is at five a.m., so when you hear the bugle sounding reveille, it's everybody up. Dismissed, except for the new arrivals."

They all scattered. We nine sweaty new arrivals waited. Cpl. Tater continued: "Find yourselves a cubicle. You'll share that cubicle with three other airmen. As soon as you've found yourself a bed there, report back here. When all of you are here, I'll take you to supply for your uniforms."

We all looked at each other and none of us said a word. Slowly we started down the hall. The barracks was a two-story wooden building. At the front end was a desk and chair where the duty officer sat. Someone in the flight was on duty at all times. Being duty officer was an eight-hour shift and everybody took her turn. Just to the left of the entry were the showers and the bathroom. As I looked at that area and identified it, I didn't know that was the last time the word "bathroom" would register whenever I saw a toilet (I quickly picked up the new word "latrine" which, I learned, was often followed by the word "duty"). My indoctrination had begun.

Adjacent to the shower area and just behind the duty officer area the cubicles began. And that's what they were. There were no doors on them. Each cubicle was separated by a wooden wall that began about a foot from the floor and ended about three feet from the ceiling. They were all painted green. I came to be fond of Air Force Blue, but I never did get a good feeling about that strange color of green.

Each cubicle held two sets of bunk beds, four foot-lockers, and four open areas each about three feet long with a pole two inches in diameter set in between. These were our very own individual clothes closets.

We could choose any cubicle that had an available bed. I moved down the hall. I don't know if I expected that the farther into the barracks I went the better the cubicles would look, or if I was simply looking for someone to be standing in the doorway ready to invite me in. Neither happened, and before I knew it I was at the last cubicle on the right. I turned to look behind me and right on my heels was another body. Luckily this last cubicle was not full. I went in and so did the gal behind me. That's how Roz and I became roommates.

Two of the bunks—the bottom ones—were apparently already taken, although the women whose stuff occupied them were not "home" at the moment. "Damn," I thought. There was no way I was going to crawl into a top bunk every night for eight weeks.

"Welcome home," I said to the gal behind me, "I'm Ret."

"Hi, Y'all. My name's Roz, from Mississippi?"

At least it sounded like a question. This was the first southern drawl I'd ever heard—and the first of many firsts for me over the next weeks and months.

Roz put her suitcase on the top bunk and I put mine on the floor. We looked at each other, shrugged our shoulders and headed back for the front of the barracks.

The rest of the new arrivals were all there waiting for us. Gathering us in tow, Cpl. Tater said, "When you've been issued your clothing, report back to the barracks, change into your fatigues, get rid of all civilian clothing or store it in the bottom of your foot locker, hang the rest of your uniform in your assigned closet area. Be sure to sign your Mess Pass after the Supply Sergeant issues it to you. Do not lose it. Your mess hall hours for dinner are 5-6:30 P.M. Not one minute before; not one minute after. I'll see you back at 1354 to answer any questions. Now follow me to Supply." I was about to have my introduction into the military way of doing things.

There was an assembly line of airmen (all women; no distinction was made between male and female) behind a long counter. Each had her specific piece(s) of clothing to issue. The first airman asked my name and started filling out the Applicable Clothing – Airman – Female Form. With her trusty tape measure, she quickly assessed me from head to toe. More often that not, an estimate was made rather than an accurate measurement.

With the "Actual Measurement" column completed, I moved to the next station. I glanced at this column as I waited my turn. I found it interesting that my bust measurement was 35. My head was 22-1/2. Doing some fast calculating I realized my head was almost 2/3 the size of my bust. Somehow that struck me as odd. At the bottom of this form was a section titled "Size Required." All pieces of the uniform were "20 Long." Since my weight at the time was 146, and I measured a layer of skin short of 5'11," I wondered how these would hang on my body.

The next airman began filling out Form DD 192 ("Organizational Clothing and Individual and Organizational Equipment Record – Enlisted Women"). She checked off the items as she handed them to me and I soon had a stack of clothing and bedding on the counter in front of me. I moved on. The next Second Lieutenant found her carbon copy of AMC Form 164C (AF Stock Fund – Clothing Division – Personal Clothing Request and Receipt) and began recording each item as she piled it on top of the already existing mound. It was all I could do to shove it down the counter to the next distribution point. I hadn't the foggiest idea how I was going to get it to the barracks.

My last stop was marked "Shortages," and this airman filled out AMC Form 164q (AF Stock Fund – Clothing Division – Female Airmen Initial Clothing Allowance Shortages). Looking at the mountain in front of me, I found it hard to believe I was missing anything. But she checked six items.

The total cost for clothing received: $149.82. Cost of clothing yet to be received: $83.90. So for a total cost of

$233.72, I had both summer and winter clothes—minus six missing pieces, and that included everyday wear, rainwear, and dress blues. As I pushed my pile of required clothing toward the end of the counter, an airman appeared from out of nowhere to help me carry it.

"Hi, I'm in 1354, too, and I'll help you get all this to your cubicle."

The only thing that would have made me happier was if she had told me she had a moving van waiting. We each took a share of the mountain and headed for "home." As we walked, she talked.

"My name's Wilma, but everybody calls me Billie. I've been here three days with nothing to do. We all had to wait until there were at least 45 girls before they assigned us a flight number. Now that you are all here we'll start our basic training tomorrow. I'm sure glad. They've been assigning us to clean the day room and police the areas around five barracks. What color are your field boots?"

"I don't know." I was real big on conversations that day.

"Well, they have to be black. The girls who came yesterday got brown ones because the black ones were all gone. And they had to dye them black. You'll have to do that, too, if yours are brown. I was lucky and got black."

My gut feeling was that I was not going to be "lucky."

"How do you dye them?"

"The supply officer brought over a whole case of black dye. The liquid kind. You put it on the boot and then burn it."

I looked at her.

"I mean you hold a match to the boot, a few inches away, and heat it. That makes the dye sink into the leather and makes it black. You have to do it twice for the boot to be real black. You gotta be careful, though, because if you don't burn it with the same amount of heat all over, parts of the boot will still be kind of brown."

Great.

"You'll have to do the same thing with the laces, only you don't have to burn them."

She laughed. I didn't.

We were at 1354. Billie dumped her load on a bottom bunk. I knew it was occupied but I thought there must be some way I could wangle that bunk and this seemed a good way to begin. So I dumped my load there, too.

"Thanks a lot, Billie."

"You're welcome. Nan helped me when I got here so now I've evened the score. I'll see you after mess call. There's a sign on the 'Notice This' board that Corporal Tater'll talk to us at 7 o'clock. If you haven't got anybody to go to the mess hall with, why don't you come with us?"

"Okay. Yeah, thanks." Like I said, I was real big on conversation that day.

"We'll stop by here and pick you up." And she was gone.

I stood looking at my new wardrobe. How could I wear this stuff? The only things that weren't wrinkled were the shoes. SHOES! I looked for the boots (at least one) to know if I had some burning to do tonight. I put my hand into the pile and blindly felt around until I grabbed onto what felt like the sole of a boot. I pulled it out and my gut feeling had been right.

I sat down on the cot, boot in hand, and wondered what I should do. I wanted the bottom bunk but knew I couldn't just take it. I couldn't hang up the clothes because which closet I used depended upon which cot I occupied. I couldn't put any of the things in the foot-locker because the locker that I would use if I could get the bottom bunk was already filled with stuff that belonged to the airman who HAD the bottom bunk. I was confident enough of my persuasive powers that I didn't want to put anything in the other locker or hang any clothes because I would just have to take them out and down. So I sat there.

"Ah'm rat heah in this firs cub'kle."

Did I recognize that voice? You bet. It was Mississippi Roz.

She came into the "cub'kle" bearing the same "gifts" I had. And right on her heels was Santa's helper whose face I could not even see. With a hefty Southern grunt she tossed her load on the bunk above mine.

The faceless airman did the same.

"This heah's Dawthy. She's jist two cub'kles away."

"Hi, Dorothy," I tried. "How long have you been here?"

Dorothy flashed a smile. "Two days." When Dorothy just stood there, there was nothing exceptional about her. But when she smiled, she sparkled.

"Thanks for heping me, hon." I discovered Roz had an irritating habit: calling everybody "hon."

With a barely audible "You're welcome," Dorothy disappeared.

"What color are your boots?" My question. I hoped everybody, or at least SOMEbody else, had brown boots.

"Aren't they all the same cullah?"

"Nope."

Roz rummaged around looking for the needle in the haystack. I watched as she pulled out a brown boot. My heart jumped for joy.

"Wal, both boots ah the sam cullah, theh brown. Whut cullah's yours?"

"Brown. And guess what?" I reiterated what Billie had told me about the dyeing and burning.

"Mah Gawd! Do we hef to do thet tanaht?"

"I guess so since Basic Training begins tomorrow. Tater'll probably tell us about it tonight."

"Yeh, seven o'clock."

Roz started shaking out her clothes, putting them on the hangers in Closet #3. They weren't as wrinkled as I expected. Mine would be if I didn't do something about the heap they were in. But I just did NOT want that upper bunk. Luckily I didn't have to think about it any more because just then our other two roommates came through the doorway.

I must have stared. I know I stared. I could feel myself staring. And there was nothing I could do about it. Through the doorway came one white girl and one black girl. In the small Wisconsin town where I grew up, there was a city ordinance that prohibited blacks from staying overnight.

They could transfer buses or change trains and if that involved a one or two hour layover, that was okay. But they could not spend the night. I never thought much about the law because there were no blacks living in the town and they were just not part of my experience. I didn't feel that I was prejudiced, but, of course, I never had an occasion to find out. As a matter of fact, I had never even seen a black up close. Now here was one walking right into the cubicle I had decided to call home for the next eight weeks. That meant I was going to see her REAL close up. That meant we would probably even undress together. And chances are it meant we might even take a shower at the same time.

"Hi," said the white girl.

"Well, looks like we've got a full house." This from the black girl.

I figured I'd take the tiger by the tail because the bottom bunk belonged to one of them. "My name's Ret," I said, creatively. "That's R-e-t."

"I'm Daphne," said the black gal, "and this is Valerie, Val, for short."

"And this is Roz, from Mississippi. Try real hard to understand her."

Instant ecstasy for Val. "Really? Ah'm from Al'bama."

Small town girl away from home for the first time and I'm surrounded by two people I can't understand and one I can't stop staring at.

"Well, wait a second," I said. "Before we start old home week here, I need to know whose bunk is under my clothes." I decided to hell with friendly persuasion. "I really don't want to sleep in an upper bunk. I'm not afraid of heights, but I usually get up during the night and when I come back to bed there's the possibility I might step right on your face or tit trying to get back up there."

The ice wasn't broken but had a major crack in it. Val broke up, Daphne hooted and Roz got red.

"The bottom bunk is mine," said Daphne.

Now what? I'd never had to bargain with a black person before and I didn't know if it was done the same as with whites or not. I mean, I didn't even know IF they bargained. My sole limited knowledge about blacks came from the movies I'd seen, the books I'd read, and Rochester on the Jack Benny show. I know enough about the suppression of the blacks to know that they still rode the back of the bus and were generally considered less than second-class citizens. If I tried to persuade Daphne to let me have the bottom bunk, would she think I was playing white supremacy with her? My mind was a jumble. And all this time I am still staring at Daphne.

"But, gosh, Ret, having the bottom bunk isn't important to me. I just took it because it was more convenient and it was available. You can have it. I'll sleep up top. I'd rather step on YOUR face and tits than you on mine," Daphne chortled.

I liked the first black girl I ever met up close and personal.

My uniforms were hung in Closet #1. I had put my Lollipops (my mother liked to buy me name-brand underwear) and my bra in the foot-locker. We had been instructed to bring six pairs of underwear and as many bras as we felt we would need. I felt I wouldn't need any, but that was not acceptable in 1951. Those items plus my garter belt were all the personal clothes we could have. Following the instructions of Daphne and Val, Roz and I rolled our underwear, bras, anklets, gloves, and duffel bag before putting them in the foot-locker. Shoes were lined up under the bottom bed; upper bunk shoes at the foot end, bottom bunk shoes at the head end.

I was still in my civilian clothes. Even though the temperature had dropped some, it was still mighty warm. I remembered Tater had said to put on our fatigues. Val and Daphne were wearing tan cotton dresses. These were fatigue dresses and were to be our daily attire. And it pleased me no end to hear that you didn't wear hose with these dresses. Just the brown anklets and field boots.

Life in Basic Training was rigid, instructive, confining, disciplined. Everything was scheduled. Up at 5 to "Fall In"

45

for Roll Call at 6, march to breakfast, back to the barracks until 8. The "Fall In" for marching drill was where we learned the fundamentals of marching: always step off with the right foot, and the left foot always hits the ground on the heavy beat of the drum. We learned that there is a difference between "by the right flank, har'ch" and "right oblique har'ch;" that "to the rear, har'ch" command was executed on the right foot; that there was a difference between the "left face, har'ch" and "right face har'ch," and that there definitely was a correct way to make an "about face." We learned the meaning of the word "cadence." There were classes to attend, information to memorize (the Articles of War), and class notes to be studied.

We never left the WAF area. If we were not in our barracks, we were outside picking up paper, cigarette butts, and any other litter we could find. When we weren't doing any of these, we were ironing our tan fatigue dresses, or washing clothes, or putting a shine on the Lil' Abners, as our boots came to be known. We were always pulling some "duty" or another for the security and cleanliness of the barracks, and always readying our cubicles for routine inspection AND those inspections that were unannounced. Discipline was primary to everything else. I didn't have much discipline growing up, yet I took to it easily. The discipline in basic training agreed with me.

I eventually came to love my Lil' Abners. I had never in my life worn boots about the ankle and so was not sure how my feet would react. I found out real fast. After the first day, the area on my leg where the top of the boot rubbed was quite tender, and the back of my heels red. At the end of three days of wear, my ankles were a mass of blisters in various stages of development. Some areas were fire red waiting for just one more rub before they were born into full-fledged blisters. Some were broken open showing the new skin red and raw. Some were filled with water waiting to burst. The remaining unblistered area was simply waiting its turn. I was not the only one. Actually, almost every woman there had the same problem.

There was no letting up, however. When we complained to Corporal Tater about our blistered feet, she said, "The only way you are going to break in the Lil' Abners is to keep wearing them. I'll send over some Band-Aids." I didn't understand how a couple of Band-Aids were going to ease the pain, but neither was I going to beg for mercy. I simply covered my heels with Band-Aids, put the Lil' Abners back on my feet, and marched. We all did. But the pain; oh, the pain. There was no way we were allowed to limp as we marched so it was just a matter of gritting our teeth and lifting one foot at a time. Corporal Tater was right, though. After about ten days, those boots were as comfortable as bedroom slippers. I took them with me to Lowry AFB in Colorado and then to McClellan AFB in Sacramento. I loved my Lil' Abners.

One of the regular occurrences during basic training was KP (Kitchen Police) duty, which we all had to "pull." During my eight weeks of Basic Training at Lackland AFB, I pulled KP three times. Two were uneventful; one was not. The eventful duty occurred when I was assigned to the Officers' Mess Hall. I discovered immediately their food was a better grade, and they had more choices of everything: entrees, vegetables, desserts, and drinks. There also were more airmen per officer to serve them, and the officers had a rotten attitude toward those on KP.

Breakfast was no problem: I was on the serving line. Lunch was a problem: I cleared the tables. Dinner was really a problem: I scraped the plates. The duty worked like this: The airman assigned to clearing the tables would bring the trays with the dirty plates and silverware and napkins and toothpicks and whatever else the officers decided to leave, to another area and set the tray contents on a long metal table. Depending upon how many officers ate at that particular meal, the pile of dirty dishes could get quite high. It was here that the airman on "plate scraping" did her work. There were several large garbage cans into which the uneaten food had to be scraped. This was my job. I knew the plates had to be scraped clean of all foods before the dishwasher got them. So

I set about my job with the same vigor I gave to all my assignments. I pulled one garbage can over closer to the metal table and began my task.

This particular dinner menu that I'll never forget began with a choice of mashed potatoes with gravy, or rice topped with some strange orangeish sauce; ham with pineapple sauce, beef with gravy, or turkey with dressing; green beans with what looked like nuts in them, or cranberry sauce with mayonnaise on top. The salad was either cottage cheese and pineapple, or regular lettuce and tomato with a choice of three dressings. Dessert was cake, pie, or ice cream in a little paper cup, or pudding. The officers could choose to drink coffee, milk, or fruit punch in a cardboard container.

As they went through the line, the officers received their silverware wrapped in a paper napkin along with a packaged toothpick. The residue of all of this was what I looked at. Undaunted, I started the scraping. It didn't take me too many plates to realize it was not necessary for me to clean these plates with my hands; I could use the used napkins. Thus I began to fill one garbage can, then a second, and a third, and I was on the fourth can when the mess sergeant came over to me, tapped me on the shoulder and motioned for me to follow him. We walked about 15 steps away from my scraping area. Then he stopped, and said to me:

"Obviously, airman, you weren't listening this morning when the duties were explained. Were you there?"

"Yes, Sir," I said. But HE wasn't. Some other sergeant was, I remembered.

"Well," he said, "you cannot scrape all the food stuffs together. They have to be separated. Now go get those trashcans and bring them out here behind the kitchen. Then you go through them all and separate all the foods from the papers and anything else that is not a food."

Was he kidding? Did he have any idea what that meant? Did he care? My flash answer to all these questions was "no." Was he serious? Yes.

He stood there and waited while I went back into the area and dragged, one at a time, the three full garbage cans and the partially filled fourth.

"Tip them over on their sides so you can get that stuff out of there easier."

I'd already thought of that. I wasn't about to bend from the waist down and burrow my head into those garbage cans.

"Get two empty cans to start separating this stuff into." *Right, you bet, asshole.* I got two empty cans.

"I'll be back," he promised. *I live for the moment, torpedo nose.*

This may have been the first moment since my enlistment when I wondered how wise my decision was to join the AF. I pulled the first can over and the garbage rolled out: mashed potatoes mixed with cottage cheese lying next to chocolate pudding surrounded by half eaten pieces of lettuce with an awful tan dressing, crumpled napkins with gravy dripping from them, toothpicks shoved into smashed tomatoes, soggy ice cream containers and half-filled milk cartons, green beans with cigarette butts standing erect, and everywhere rice with some strange orangeish sauce.

I knew if I put my hands into that garbage can to bring out the paper goods, the toothpicks, and the cigarette butts, I would throw up. Saliva was forming in my mouth at an exceedingly fast rate and I was trying to keep pace with it by continually swallowing.

"You'd better get busy, Airman, it'll be dark soon and then you'll be doing this by flashlight." Torpedo nose had returned. He didn't say this with any tone of compassion, rather it had a ring of threat combined with "and you'd better believe it." Then he turned and walked away.

I spent the next hour and fifteen minutes working at a frantic pace. There were times when my whole body down to my knees was inside that garbage can. And those were the moments when saliva flowed most freely and I swallowed most rapidly. I finished just as dusk began to give way to dark.

I knew what I must have looked like. I wondered if the sergeant was going to come back to check the cans. I wondered, but I didn't wait to find out. When I got back to the barracks, there were a few inquiries as to where I'd been. I answered them with an unintelligible grunt, took a shower, and went to bed. When I awoke the next morning, my mouth had no saliva in it. My mouth stayed dry for three full days.

CHAPTER FIVE:

ORDERS

The days became weeks as we continued to attend various classes. We learned how to identify airplanes (ours and the enemy's). We got lessons in quickly affixing our gas mask in the event of a gas war (this included the final survival test when we were marched, squad by squad, into a closed room, exposed to gas, and blindly had to put on our masks). And always we were marching, marching, marching. We were drilled to perfection so that on graduation day when all the airmen (male and female) participated in parading before the Commanding Officer of the Base our flight would be able to "move as one giant body" as Corporal Tater put it.

As we neared the end of our eight weeks of basic training, we began to wonder what our aptitude test had revealed about us. All the women had taken an aptitude test during the beginning of our training, and those test results would determine what our specific jobs would be and where we would spend the next two months learning that job. We were scheduled to graduate on the Friday of the eighth week, and those who had their orders would leave immediately the following Monday.

Tearful good-byes began upon the arrival of the first orders. I had never been away from home before my enlistment, and had not made intimate friends I'd had to bid farewell. I had also never encountered the death of a meaningful family member. So I was ill-equipped to deal with partings. There was an intense closeness that had occurred during the eight weeks with those other women.

Oh, not with all of them. But there were several women I had grown very close to and felt a real loss knowing they were going to be sent to a different part of the U.S.

I guess it wasn't unusual for a certain intimacy to develop when I spent every moment of every day for eight weeks with the same people. We did latrine duty together, showered in open showers together, shared our deodorant and our dollars, traded tasks and favors, listened to each other and gave support to each other, and probably most important, we laughed together. I imagine there are some people who feel that becoming too close and then parting is so painful they would not do it again. My feeling is just the opposite: this closeness had brought so much into my life that even though the parting caused an ache in my heart, I looked forward to developing more close friendships.

Finally I received my orders. I was assigned to Lowry AFB in Denver, Colorado, for training as a Machine Accountant. I had no idea what that was and anyone I asked had no idea, either. I wasn't disappointed with the assignment because there was no particular area I was intent upon entering. It would have been nice to know what I would be learning, but it was no big deal. But the place! Colorado! Cripes, they had more snow than Wisconsin and I was going there in the middle of winter. However, even that didn't really faze me. I was totally accepting of wherever they wanted to send me. I was just excited about being in the Air Force. And besides, it was a temporary assignment.

After the graduation exercises, we were all promoted to A/3C (Airman Third Class, one stripe). Of course, all during basic training the threat was constantly there that if I did not do this well, or failed to do that properly, I would not be given my stripe. It must have worked, because we all received our first stripe. Five of us sat up that night sewing them on. We had to have them on all our clothing, and that's a lot of sewing. Plus, all the sewing had to be done by hand. My stitching took considerably more time than the others,' but when I was finished it was the prettiest thing I'd seen. I loved my uniform. And with a stripe on it, it was a sensation to behold!

There were a number of other women from Lackland assigned to Lowry, and we took solace in that. Arrival date was 1 December, with a reporting date of 2 December. That made it necessary for us to leave as soon after graduation as possible, depending on what sort of transportation we could manage. We were not on flying status, but authorization had been given to fly commercially or to travel by bus or rail. We chose rail (I loved the train).

Our accommodations at Lowry Air Force Base were different from those at Lackland. Instead of the four-person cubicles, the barracks was "open bay." That is, there was a row of bunk beds down each side of the barracks with clothing space at the head of each bed. So much for privacy. If any of us had any inhibitions left they would be taken care of now.

This open bay arrangement didn't bother me. It never bothered me to undress in front of other women. And for that I'm grateful; especially when I saw the extremes to which some of the women would go to hide their nakedness while getting dressed. The most commonly used method was to drape the bath towel in front of the body so that the top end was snug up to the neck and then hold it in place with the chin. As long as the body was erect, there was no problem. But the minute the woman bent over (as in the process of putting on her underwear), although the towel still hung straight down, it was now about 10-12 inches from her body. The other problem with this method of cover-up was that if someone spoke, it was practically impossible to answer them.

Machine Accountant School was, by today's definition, a computer school and, I believe, one of the first. We began training on IBM machines. Learning to operate key punch machines came first. There we learned not only how to put the information on the key punch cards, but to sight read them as well. Then came training in wiring the machine boards to do what we wanted them to do. With the wiring techniques under our belt, we began our education in the operation of the actual machines.

The first was a huge monster, the Tabulator. Even though this was its official name, everyone called it by its number, the 402. This was the machine that printed the information onto the continuously fed paper. After we had key punched the information on the IBM cards, wired the boards to tell the 402 what information we wanted printed from the cards, placed the cards in the holder and fed the paper into the machine, the big 402 rumbled into action. There was no mistaking the sound of this machine. I always knew when someone was operating it. The other machines operated at half the volume and were all called by name.

They did exactly what their name indicated. The "Interpreter" would interpret the punched information and print it on the top of the card. The "Multiplier" would make as many duplicates of the card as you asked it to. The "Collator" would shuffle the cards and put them together in any manner I wanted (this information was told to the machine by the board I wired). And the "Sorter" would sort the cards alphabetically or numerically. This last machine was the one that caused most of the trouble. Often the cards would jam, get crinkled or have edges cut. This meant I had to go back to the key punch machine and start all over.

I liked this training and the instructor assured us this was the future right before our eyes; that these machines would ultimately be in common usage. He convinced us that if we successfully completed our training, we would be one step ahead of civilians in this area. Hence, if and when we decided to leave the military, we would have no problem finding employment. He was certain these machines would be at the mast of most every major business.

Now when I think about the widespread use of computers, their portability and their infinite capabilities, I realize how right he was. I successfully completed my training and figured I was one step ahead of my civilian counterparts. But there, for me, the truth of his statement ended. I was never able to use that training later.

On 21 February 1952, I completed my training at Lowry AFB and received a Certificate of Proficiency in Machine Accounting. I also received two sets of orders. The first order granted me fifteen days leave, and the second was the notification of where I would be permanently stationed.

I anticipated this second set of orders with mixed emotions. One of the forms we had completed while still in basic training had asked the question where we would like to be permanently based. Reaching for the moon, I wrote my choices as California, Hawaii, and Florida, in that order. I didn't know if the Great Airman in the Sky paid any attention to my wishes or not, but if she did I wanted mine to be known. But when it came right down to it, it really didn't make any difference where they sent me. I was a happy airman.

So when orders came through that I was to be sent to California, I was ecstatic. Having spent all my life in Wisconsin, the pot at the end of the rainbow was California. And I was going to be stationed there on a permanent basis. The Goddess was smiling on me!

I decided to use the fifteen days leave to go to Wisconsin and pick up my car, a green 1937 Chevy I affectionately named the Green Hornet. It would be great to have my car again. The month of March in Colorado is a lot like the month of March in Wisconsin: cold, windy, snowy. I bundled up in my AF blues and took the train to Appleton. I will say one thing for the winter uniforms; they were warm. Even though the overcoat was heavy and bulky, it kept me toasty. At least the winter blues I had been issued were my size; contrary to the array of sizes I had received in basic training.

My sister Irene, her husband Mark, and their three boys were living in Appleton at this time, and they had talked periodically about relocating some place with warmer winters. When I saw them in March and mentioned that I'd like to drive my car back to Sacramento, Mark said, "Well, maybe we can strike up a deal. I'd like to take a look at that area and you want your car out there. How about if I help you drive back? That way I can save bus fare and you'll have somebody to ride with. Then I can take the bus back home."

That sounded like a peach of an idea to me. We went over to my sister Bette's where I had stashed the car in the backyard the previous October. There it stood in about 2-1/2 feet of snow. Every flat surface and ledge was covered with snow, and crusty ice had formed on the windshield. Mark said that since I hadn't had any problems with the car it probably just needed a new battery. He was right. After breaking the icy seal on the hood, Mark installed the new battery. Then he cleaned enough snow off the door area to be able to open the door. He got in, pumped the accelerator a few times, turned the key, and after only a couple of grinds, the motor roared. Wonderful!

And so it came to pass that Mark and I drove from Appleton, Wisconsin, to Sacramento, California, in the middle of March in my 1937 Chevy which, incidentally, was hitting only seven of its eight cylinders for half the trip. I remember the beauty of the country as we drove West along Highway 80. Snowflakes as big as silver dollars were falling lightly as we began the climb over Donner Pass. I was amazed at the amount of snow that had already fallen. At the ski lodges, buildings were totally covered with snow. Tunnels had been shoveled from the road to the entrance of the buildings and about all that could be seen were smoking chimneys and groups of skis standing in the snow where some brave skier had stuck them. Some areas had been cleared for parking, but few had cars in them.

I dropped Mark off at the Greyhound Bus Depot in Sacramento and drove to McClellan Air Force Base, which was just a few miles outside the city. As I showed my orders to the Air Police at the base gate, was given the "go-ahead" and drove onto the base, I felt as though my life were starting anew. I had the plan all mapped out in my mind. This was the beginning of a successful career in the "service." I knew that if I were a good airman, I would achieve my goal. But I intended to be better than a good airman. I intended to be an outstanding airman and move up the ladder of promotion as quickly as the regulations allowed. I would accomplish this by my exemplary work habits and job performance, by paying strict attention to the military rules, by my positive attitude, enthusiastic spirit, and dedication to my country. I would take advantage of educational courses where I could earn college credit and even graduate with a degree. I would be active in sports; I would establish myself as a regular blood donor; I would be a part of as many alternate programs as I could. I believed this without exception. There was never a doubt in my mind that I had found a home in the Air Force. How naïve of me; how trusting of me.

I was assigned to work the regular day shift in the Personnel and Maintenance Building. There I applied all the skills I had learned at Machine Accountant School and my life in the military became routine. Six weeks later, I was assigned to swing shift, and ultimately to graveyard. Although I didn't particularly like going to work at midnight, that shift was the best because it was only seven hours. Also, there was less confusion and fewer people to contend with. And it was great during the hot summer months.

In October my military supervisor submitted a recommendation to change my primary AFS (Air Force Specialty) from an apprentice machine accountant to a senior machine accountant. This meant nothing as far as promotion was concerned but it did indicate I had successfully completed the OJT (On the Job Training). It also meant I was capable of performing more advanced tasks.

So, I was transferred to the day shift to work in the Personnel and Aircraft Section, Statistical Services Division, under both a military supervisor and a civilian supervisor. There I had a variety of duties that included the control, audit, and processing of statistical reports relative to personnel, using the proto-computers. I also had the opportunity to work in Personnel and often served as an alternate for the Personnel Rep, and assisted in Defense Bond Sales. All of these I performed to the best of my abilities and with a great deal of pride.

I had a great relationship with the civilian women at work. Often I would be invited to dinner at their homes, and frequently to spend a weekend. Since they lived off base, this was a special treat.

Speaking of pride, I was filled with it when we marched in the Memorial Day parade in 1952 through downtown Sacramento. This was my first and only off-base parade. The only other marching I had done since basic training was when VIP's would visit the base, or when there would be an awards ceremony. Even then, marching on the base to Sousa's "Stars and Stripes Forever," and hearing the commands "Pass in Review," and "Eyes Right," always made me feel special—one-of-a-kind, hand-picked.

But marching in that parade with the sidewalks lined deep with people and all of them cheering, and the Air Force band right ahead playing "Under the Double Eagle," was just about more than I could take. I think I had the same intensity about Sousa's music, the military, and military marching as General Patton did about battle. God, how I loved it!

I joined the basketball team and we had a winning season like never before in the history of the base. I reveled in the camaraderie and the beginning of friendships that went beyond any I had experienced before. We were an extended family, part of which was always there. We did so much together: showered, ate meals, celebrated too much. We confided in each other. What we did not do was sleep together. We all knew the rules and, except for an instance or two unrelated to me, none of us shared a bed on base.

From basketball to softball, same group, same camaraderie. I could feel myself finding a place in the hearts of these Air Force women, and in the soul of the Air Force itself.

My life was following the plan perfectly. I couldn't have suspected that one incoming phone call at work in May 1953 would be the beginning of the end of it all. Yet, when the phone rang and my supervisor Russella said it was for me, I was startled. No one ever called me at work. And so it was with apprehension, curiosity, and downright fear that I answered the phone.

The female voice on the other end said, "Airman Coller, will you please come to Building 3, and come immediately?" I said ok and then she asked, "Do you know where it is?" I did and I told her so. After I hung up, I told Russella I had to report to another building right away. No problem. Over the next months, I wondered what Russella thought when the phone would ring so frequently and I would have to leave. She never said a word to me about it.

I walked into Building 3 and identified myself to the female sergeant behind the desk. She then disappeared through a door. Very soon she reappeared followed by a man who introduced himself as Ben from the OSI (Office of Special Investigation). He flashed me a badge. "Let's go in here," he said as he pointed to the doorway he had just come from. I followed him into an anteroom of sorts where two other men sat. Ben introduced these men as OSI agents Al and Harold. They motioned for me to sit down. And thus began my first interrogation session with the OSI.

Up until that moment Building 3 had been just another building on the base, same color as all the rest and deceivingly innocent looking. An hour later it had become, for me, a chamber of horrors that haunted the rest of my time in the Air Force.

CHAPTER SIX:

BETRAYAL

Ben sat to my right about three feet away, Al sat to my left at the same distance, and directly across from me sat the agent introduced as Harold. Each had a specific duty. It was Ben's responsibility to ask the questions, Al's to write down the verbal responses, and Harold's to watch and record my non-verbal reactions. The tenor of this first meeting was quickly established by Ben.

"Do you know why you are here?"

"No."

"You have no idea why we want to talk to you?"

"No."

"Do you know any other airmen we have talked to?"

"No." This last "No" was the first of thousands of answers that I gave over the next months that were to be untruthful. I did know that Georgianna, naturally called "George" by her friends, had been a frequent visitor to Building 3. We played basketball together on McClellan's WAF team and were a vital part of the WAF softball team. We had lifted many a beer together and had a great time playing one-upmanship.

George had an incredible capacity when it came to beer drinking. More often than not she was the last one standing. She was also the happiest drunk I've ever known. Frequently, when she was in one of these "states," she would drop over to Building 3, ask to talk to an OSI agent, and promptly confess to an assortment of "abnormal sexual activities." From somewhere in the depths of her soul there lived a germ of caution because she never signed anything and never involved anyone else by name. And usually the next day she would be visited by two OSI men who would escort her to the "room" in Building 3 and ask her to reiterate her statements of the day before.

She would calmly tell them she had no memory whatsoever of saying anything to them. She had been drinking and was certainly not in any condition to be responsible for what she had said or done. I had never been called to testify that George had, indeed, been out drinking. But I knew those who had.

"Well, Airman Coller, you are here because you are associating with women we believe to be homosexuals and, as you know, it is stated in Article 35-66, that homosexuals are unfit to serve in the Armed Forces and are subject to discharge. What we'd like to do today is just ask you a few questions."

I did not respond. I know he didn't need my permission to ask a few questions and I decided right then I was going to answer his questions in as few words as possible. I tried my best to keep a blank look on my face while still coming across as semi-intelligent. I also knew, at that moment, the meaning of fear.

No words crossed my mind to define it but the feeling that permeated my body and caused me to feel nauseous could be nothing else. Up until this time, I had been looking directly at Ben. Now I took a moment to look Harold squarely in the eyes. Somehow I wanted him to know that I was secure in who I was, and I felt I could best accomplish this by direct eye contact.

The moment I looked into his eyes I knew why he had the job of observing reactions. Although his whole demeanor was one of non-intimidation, his stare was totally accusatory. In his eyes I saw determination and damnation, assurance and abhorrence, and the confidence of conviction. I found it impossible to believe those eyes could reflect any other feeling than contempt--and that belief was with me until the day I was escorted off McClellan AF base.

"Where is your home, Airman Coller?"

With that question, we began a review of my entire life: birthplace, parents, siblings, education, who my friends were, my extra-curricular activities, my grades and favorite subjects, favorite teachers, leisure time (how much and how I filled it), hobbies, books, special places, favorite clothes, friends (more female than male?), jobs, interests, goals. After the trip down memory lane, Ben asked about my current social life.

"How do you spend your free time on the base?"

That was a strange question because I really didn't have that much "free" time on the base. I now worked the day shift, 7:30 – 4:30, and after dinner I spent time doing the same things everyone else did: visiting, reading, getting clothes ready for the next day, writing letters.

Weekends we sometimes went off the base. Much of what we did was determined by the AF. Often there were on-base parades on the weekends, basketball or softball games, on-base duties and unannounced inspections. I wasn't quite sure how to answer that question so I gave it my best shot.

"Just doing the regular things."

"And what are those?"

I gave him a rundown of what a typical week was like. He seemed satisfied and then asked:

"Do you date any men on the base?"

"No."

"Don't you think that's a bit unusual?"

"No."

"Do you think about dating men?"

"No."

"Don't you think that's a bit unusual?"

"Well, I haven't thought about it because I haven't seen anyone I would like to date."

"Do you know if any of the airmen in your barracks are dating men?"

"Yes, Nancy has a steady boyfriend, Barb has been going out with this one fellow, a civilian, for a couple of months, and Sarah dates her boss."

"How about George? Does she date any men? Or what about Helen, or Anne or Jean?"

"I don't know anything about them; I don't know if they date men or not."

"Do you know if any of these airmen are homosexuals?"

"No."

"Have any of them ever talked to you about homosexuality?"

"No."

"Do you spend a lot of time with them?" George, Helen, Anne and Jean played basketball and softball and we did our share of socializing together. So I know he had the answer to that question before I opened my mouth.

"Quite a bit."

"And out of all that time you spend together, homosexuality was never mentioned?"

"No." God, he just wouldn't quit.

"Well, Airman Coller, that's all for now. If you notice any homosexual behavior in your barracks, or in any other barracks, or if you think someone might be homosexual, I hope you will tell us. We would never mention you told us and it would look good on your record if you could help us."

I didn't say a word.

"You can go."

As I got up to leave, I realized my whole body felt different. The fear that had been so prevalent in the beginning was gone. There was another feeling that encompassed me now. It was anger. I was furious. With each step that took me out of the anteroom, across the office and through the outer door, the anger grew. By the time I reached the barracks I was livid.

I really believed this interrogation would have no bearing on my career. So it was with surprise that I responded to the OSI's invitation to Building 3 four more times.

It was common knowledge at McClellan AFB—common, that is, to the personnel I worked with, as well as to my Commanding Officer, that my office skills were above average. I could type a rapid 80 wpm. I had an innate sense of time management. I could create and prioritize new systems incorporated into an office. I'm certain that's why, even though I was under investigation by the OSI, Major Brunski recommended me for an important assignment: to help a Colonel—Colonel Couch, set up the ROTC Summer Camp that was to begin operation at McClellan within a few weeks.

Even though I had experienced several weeks of investigation by the OSI, I had steadfastly maintained my innocence. I was able to do so in large part because of the support of the other women. Had I been left to depend on my own stamina, I probably would have submitted long before. Now, however, my personnel file had been red-flagged. I was not qualified to be promoted. If and when I was ever re-assigned, the investigative information in my file would follow me. So it was that Major Brunski had to inform Colonel Couch of my status. The Colonel was not deterred, and three days later I was summoned to the CO's office, introduced to Colonel Couch, and given the ROTC assignment.

The office for the ROTC was set up in one of the empty barracks across the road in the Male Personnel area. This area was fenced and bore several large signs stating "Off Limits to Female Personnel." I felt a certain sense of importance as I walked through the gates displaying the pass Colonel Couch had written and signed for me.

In one half of the empty barracks stood numerous pieces of furniture. Male personnel had been garnered from some unsuspecting unit and, under the direction of Colonel Couch, began to set up the ROTC office. I looked at the Colonel who had ignored my investigative status. Tall, grey haired, slender and soft-spoken, he epitomized my idea of a successful career officer.

For one month and one day I worked with Colonel Couch and his officer subordinates. During that period of time, I was not bothered once by the OSI. The phone never rang summoning me to Building 3. My mail seemed to be untouched. And I ate every meal without interference. My nights were uninterrupted and I began to fantasize that perhaps the inquiry had ended.

In late July Major Brunski summoned me to her office. I had had few reasons to appear before her, and since the OSI had not bothered with me for several weeks, I felt quite certain it had nothing to do with them. After exhibiting the proper military protocol, she told me to sit down. Then she spoke to me about the ROTC Summer Camp, Col. Couch's appreciation for the good job I had done--including making the new ROTC candidates feel at home, my dependability, my willingness to learn and to work extra hours, my initiative and my abilities. She ended this bouquet of roses by telling me that Colonel Couch had submitted to her a recommendation for my promotion to A/1C (3 stripes: a Sergeant!). She then went on to say that it was her sad duty to tell him that since I was under investigation, no promotions were possible.

Colonel Couch still did what he could: he wrote a Letter of Appreciation with the desire that it be placed in my 201 file. Major Brunski added a letter to the bottom of Colonel Couch's stating what a credit I was to the Women of the Air Force. Five months later I was given an Undesirable Discharge.

Trusting had always been easy for me; probably because I had had rare occasion in my life not to trust. I was soon to discover that the place trust had always held was now to be shared with suspicion.

For that reason, I later understood the actions of my friends upon my return to the barracks after my first visit with the OSI. Through my anger I heard their questions: "Did they ask about me?" Their first question wasn't "What did they want?" They already knew that. Now they were concerned about what had transpired. "Did I mention any of their names? Did I confess to anything? Sign anything? Did I have to go back? Were there questions about the ball teams? Did they know where we went when we were in town? Were any questions asked about the women at Mather AFB? Did they have any papers or letters I had written?"

I couldn't believe my friends thought for one minute that I would give those men any information about their personal lives. Why would I do that? It was inconceivable and for a moment added to my anger. Still, I answered all their questions, and there was noticeable relief when they heard my answers. I wondered why they were all so worried. We had talked about the OSI, the McCarthy inquiries, and the purges on other Air Force bases. We had noted the fact that McClellan had so far escaped any investigations, but when they began we kept a mental record of which of us had been summoned for questioning and how each handled it. The fact that we needed to bond together and maintain a silence had been discussed countless times.

Now my friends had doubted my ability to handle my first session. Two days later, when Jean returned to the barracks after a two-hour probe by the agents, I understood. I found myself among the group of women waiting anxiously outside the barracks door for Jean to appear. Suspicion and fear filled my mind as I wondered if she would be able to withstand the pressure of the repetitious questions, the innuendoes, the accusations and the eyes. That afternoon very little was said as the five of us sat on the steps in the fading sun. The scant dialogue intimated our concerns and our doubts.

"How many times is this for Jean?" someone asked.

George, probably the calmest of all for having the most experience at this, said it was too many to count. "After the first half dozen times, you lose track. What's the point? It's not like there's a maximum number of times they'll come get you and after that you don't have to worry anymore."

We all knew she was right, and even though it was a moot point, it paved the way for conversation. "Do those guys really believe any of us will ever give them any information?" This came from Helen, the First Sergeant who, at the moment, was having an affair with George. She, too, was an old hand at dealing with the OSI. Even though the investigations at McClellan had begun only a short time before, she was in it from the outset. As First Sergeant she spent most of her time at headquarters behind a desk doing whatever it is First Sergeants did.

I learned, however, that any time a WAF was called to Building 3, she joined the group that waited. It wasn't always the same group. There were those who believed some OSI agent was stationed behind an adjacent building taking notes on who comprised the group, and so always to be seen keeping vigil was a sure sign of guilt. Their reasoning was that there would be no concern unless there was something to be concerned about. The first time I heard that I pooh-poohed it saying I couldn't conceive a grown man lurking behind the barracks or peering around the corner just to see who was sitting on the steps. That kind of behavior was found only in Humphrey Bogart movies. I later learned that nothing was beyond the scope of these agents. They had a mission: to rid McClellan AFB of all the homosexuals. And to accomplish that mission they know no bounds. Helen knew all this, yet she kept as many vigils as her duties would allow.

"I suppose they figure they'll get to us through each other. That if they keep this up some of us will crack. But I know it won't be Jean." PeeWee said this in the same tone she used when someone asked her if she thought we'd win the softball game. PeeWee was the scorekeeper, too pudgy to run yet determined to be involved somehow and always predicting us to win.

"Do they ask everybody the same questions?" I was curious. This was all new for me and I needed some answers. "Do the same three guys always have the interrogation?"

"As far as we can tell, there are five OSI guys here. At least these same five guys have been here since I got here." Matt hadn't been interrogated since last month but was one of the "originals." "I've had four of them and they're all bastards."

George spoke up. "They make it a policy to always have at least one guy be the same one with you every time. I guess they figure that makes you more comfortable. And there's always three. The only time that changes is when I get smashed and go over there. That always takes them by surprise." She didn't seem to mind the fact that she'd give them a drunken confession and then recant. As a matter of fact, I think she rather enjoyed it.

"Sure, they keep asking the same questions over and over. Sometimes they put new ones in and often they'll lie to you just to see if they can get you to give them a name. The thing is, they've got nothing on any of us. We haven't done anything on base and as long as we stay tight and don't give them a name, we'll be ok. They can't discharge us just for playing softball or basketball, for Christ's sake!"

Maybe not, but they could get us other ways.

At first I didn't even know I was under investigation. I thought I was being questioned along with a lot of other women just so the OSI could get as much information as possible. I hadn't done anything on base to arouse their suspicions; I knew better than to get involved with anyone in the service. I was, however, involved with a gal living in Sacramento.

I had met Marie and her sister the previous fall. Both of them were lesbians and we became fast friends. They were of Hungarian descent and neither of the parents spoke fluent English. Her parents liked me immediately, and I spent free weekends between their house and Marie's sister's home. I would take the bus into Sacramento on Friday afternoon; one of them would pick me up, and I'd return Sunday evening. They were all extremely good to me--even Marie's brothers. They opened their home and made me a part of the family. My involvement with Marie was honest, relatively intense, short-lived, and always off the base. I would never have done anything to hurt any of them; yet, in the act of saving myself, I submitted to doing the one thing in my life that I regret.

It didn't take me long to realize I was one of the focal points of the OSI in their effort to purge McClellan AFB. Often I would be in the middle of a meal and they would march right into the mess hall, up to my table, and off I would go with them to another question and answer session.

68

Often these never lasted longer than 15-20 minutes; it was the constant interruptions any time and place that began to plague me.

They came to my room looking for anything they believed would be incriminating. They found my Air Force picture album and took it. At the next interrogation they put in front of me pictures that had been taken from my album. I couldn't believe it! I was incensed! Just who did these guys think they were? They not only took my album—and took it without my permission—but they ripped nine pictures out of it!

And then they had the gall to shove them one by one in my face and ask me if I could see anything "abnormal, different, unusual, not quite right," about them. After I said "no" to all their insipid questions, I asked for my pictures and my album. Their response was that I could have the album, but they needed to keep the pictures "for awhile." I didn't see those pictures again until December.

They just didn't quit. They confiscated and read my mail. Most embarrassing of all, they frequently called me at work. The phone would ring and the minute my supervisor looked at me and handed me the phone, I knew who it was—and so did she. I would have to leave work immediately, go to Building 3 and make it through another session.

The sessions were pretty much all the same. They wanted to know if I was a homosexual, if there were any other airmen I associated with who were homosexuals, what did I do for sexual outlet, why did I not date men, did we have parties, what did we do at those parties, what did I know about so-and-so.

I was slowly reaching the point where these interrogations were seriously affecting my stability. It was difficult for me to concentrate at work; every time the phone rang my whole body reacted. Meals were difficult; I never knew if I'd be able to finish without interruption. And there seemed to be no end in sight. This was not a four- or six-month investigation after which I'd just move on to another base. This was here to stay. Rather than my getting used to this harassment, becoming flexible and able to incorporate it into my life as many of the other women were able to do, I felt myself becoming more and more fragile.

During the last few times I was questioned, the men of the OSI had told me that if I didn't want to incriminate any other airman, I could simply admit my own homosexuality and I would get a General Discharge from the service. This would not be a black mark on my record, since this type of discharge was given for other reasons such as women getting married or pregnant. I began seriously to consider this as the only viable option. These OSI men were really good at their job.

"You must see that your staying in the AF could only be detrimental to the service. You are a security risk since anyone disloyal to our country could blackmail you into giving them important information. You are, as are your homosexual friends, a threat to the security of our country."

I had no idea, in the wildest of my ideas, how I could be a security risk. I had no security clearance, so I had no access to anything secret. I wasn't assigned to any ranking officer. For what could I be blackmailed?

Up until a month or so before this, I didn't need any help. Now I wasn't so sure. Feeling less and less able to cope, the idea of a General Discharge and release from this constant questioning became more appealing. Finally, when I knew that it was a matter of my keeping a hold on my sanity, I went to my CO, Major Brunski, and asked for her advice.

"I'm thinking of going to the OSI and telling them about me. I just can't handle this anymore. What do you think?" I knew I was putting her on the spot, but I needed some direction from someone who could think clearly. She was very aware of all that was going on and, I felt, wanted to do what she could to help me.

She put her arms on her desk and leaned forward. "If you feel that's what you have to do, then do it. But please think carefully about what you are doing." She looked at me. "This will affect you the rest of your life, you know."

No, I didn't know. I had no idea of the impact it would have on the rest of my life. And, frankly, the rest of my life was not even a consideration at this point. I was 22. The rest of my life was somewhere between oblivion and obscurity. How could I deal with the rest of my life when I couldn't deal with one day?

Major Brunski spoke in an almost motherly tone to me: "Why don't you go back to your barracks, let a day or two pass, and see if you still feel the same. If you do, then you can act." That sounded like a good idea to me, and I told her so, then thanked her and left.

That night I talked to Carol. She had been going through pretty much the same thing I was, and was just about at the same point, emotionally. I told here about my visit with Major Brunski, and Carol wanted to know if I felt any different than I had felt that morning. No, I didn't. Well, neither did she. She'd been thinking about doing the same thing. The next day, she said, she would. Me, too. We pretty much made up our minds right there. We decided it would be easier for each of us to do this thing together. The following day we both went to the Orderly Room and individually spoke to Major Brunski.

When I told Major Brunski of my decision, she said, "I hope you have given this ample thought. You have a good record, and I'd like to see you try to stay in the Air Force."

I told her I couldn't. I just wasn't strong enough to cope with this kind of pressure. She stood up and came around to the front of her desk. She took my hand and said, "I wish you all the best then, Ret."

She had never called me that before. It was usually just the last name she used. I sensed sadness from her that now, years later, I can understand. That sadness comes from knowing what lies ahead for someone else and not being able to tell them because one's own security was at risk.

I waited while Carol went in to see the Major, and then we both walked right over to Building 3. As we walked, I felt some relief in knowing that I had made a decision. I had no concern whether it was the right one or not. A decision had been made. I felt that now I had some control.

I had to wait a few minutes while the OSI agents were summoned to their office. When two of them had arrived, the three of us went into a small conference room.

"What's so important, Airman Coller?"

"I want to make a statement. You said that if I confessed, I would get a General Discharge. Isn't that right?"

"Absolutely." This confirmation came from both of them simultaneously.

"OK, then," I said, "I'll sign a statement saying I'm a homosexual, but I won't involve any other military personnel."

"That's perfectly all right," the one with the notepad said. "Let's get your statement. Just tell it to us in your own words."

I must have looked really stupid—and in a sense, I guess I was. I thought I would just sign a "statement" saying I was a homosexual. Now I learned that I would have to tell them a STORY about being a homosexual. I just stood there.

"I'll ask you some questions if that will help you get started."

And so he did. When he finished we had a short capsule of my life and homosexual thoughts, feelings, and activities. Next he told me I would be able to get a General Discharge only if I would involve another person. This took me by complete surprise and angered me.

"That's not what you said before. You said I just needed to make a statement."

He said that giving information of homosexual activity with another girl would give validity to my statement. Then he added, "We know you've been seeing a girl in town because we have followed you on several occasions."

I couldn't believe it! FOLLOWED ME? They were that serious about getting us out of the military. "Oh, we don't know her name, but we do know where she lives."

I told him I didn't want to involve anyone else. Again he pointed out the necessity of having evidence of someone involved with me. I had thought this was going to be so simple. I could just walk in, declare my homosexuality, sign a statement to that effect and be given a General Discharge. It had taken just about all the strength I had to make that decision, now I had to make another one. And this one involved Marie.

"If I do tell you about Marie and me, what will you do?"

"Not a thing," the blonde agent said. "We have no interest in her at all. Our only interest is in you as an Airman and as a security risk."

I had to make sure. "You won't ask her any questions or anything?"

"No. We have no jurisdiction over civilians. We only have jurisdiction over military personnel."

I believed them. In my confused, hassled mind, what they said made sense. And so I gave them Marie's name and address, a story of our relationship that was both truth and truth embellished, and I added Marie's sister's address for good measure.

Knowing I was capable of compromising my values added another dimension to the ongoing anguish. I had done all this almost in a hypnotic state and when he handed me the pen to sign the paper, I had my first moment of semi-reality. I felt nauseous. I felt guilty. I felt like a traitor. I felt a sense of urgency to get to a phone and tell Marie what I had done. I felt relief.

Word of the decision Carol and I had made spread swiftly throughout the base. Within a day, we had only each other for company. Intellectually I could understand why none of our friends wanted to take a chance on being seen with us, but emotionally it cut deep. To be avoided, shunned, was devastating.

In October, a Board of Officers convened to "hear" my case. This was short and swift and, I later learned, probably violated my fundamental legal rights.

In December the decision came down from the SAF that I be "administratively discharged UP AFR 35-66 (Discharge of Homosexuals – Class II) and issued an Undesirable Discharge Certificate."

I was given no explanation for the Undesirable Discharge rather than the General Discharge I had been promised. When I tried to get an answer from the OSI men, they were never available. No one else had any information. I knew what the answer was anyway. They had lied to me. Whatever it took to get me to sign that statement was what they were capable of doing. They had questioned me until I was near emotional collapse, then they tempted me with a respectable way out, lied to me until I fell to that temptation, then they lied again. And no one on this Air Force base was going to admit that.

It took me a while to clear the base. I had to check out with the Flight Surgeon and the Chaplain, and the Provost Marshall's office (where I had to turn in my ID card, my mess card, and my base badge). Then came a trip to Payroll (where I was given a check for $56.34 for bus fare back to the origin of my enlistment), and Clothing (where I had to return every single piece of military clothing, including my Lil' Abners).

God, how I hated to give those up! I don't know what they represented for me; I only knew I wanted to keep them. I even asked the airman in Clothing if I could take them with me. Her response, dripping with disgust, was, "Not a chance, Undesirables get nothing." She had no idea how right she was.

Yet another trip awaited me to Records, where I was given a folder containing my Undesirable Discharge Certificate, Discharge Orders, and Form DD214 (Report of Separation from the Armed Forces of the United States). There a First Sergeant told me that I would be leaving the base at 2 PM that afternoon. That was the first I knew that I would not be able to leave at my own discretion. My departure time had already been determined by the OSI and the Provost Marshall.

Carol and I packed our few civilian clothes, and as we exited the barracks at 1:45, four Air Police met us at the door--two for Carol and two for me. With an AP on each side of me, I was escorted off McClellan Air Force Base on 15 December 1953.

I had walked onto Lackland AFB in October 1951 a happy, healthy, well-integrated, patriotic and career-oriented woman. Two years and two months later, the Air Force military police escorted me off McClellan Air Force Base stripped of all things military and of the one thing that makes a being human and stable—an ego. I left there disintegrated, disillusioned, distrustful and destroyed.

PART THREE:

FALLOUT, 1953-69

CHAPTER SEVEN:

GOING HOME

Carol and I stood outside the gates of the base, suitcases in hand, and waited for the bus that would take us into Sacramento. We had decided we would go to Portland, Oregon, where her parents lived and try to get things together. Although Carol and I had gone through the investigation, hearing, and discharge together, I knew we didn't have much else in common. Going with her to Portland was a haven for me at the time and a place to have a few days to consider what I wanted to do. Neither of us spoke as we waited, each of us with our own sets of thoughts on what had transpired the previous weeks.

My feeling of relief knowing there would be no more questions, no more lies, no more embarrassing phone calls, and no more tests of endurance filled me to the point that whatever tomorrow held for me seemed unimportant. When I did have a fleeting thought of the future, I had no fears I would be totally self-sufficient. I had always been and could see no reason why the same wouldn't be true now. How little I knew! How naïve I was to think this experience with the military would leave me unscathed.

I stayed in Portland with Carol and her parents for three weeks. Then I knew I had to make a move. I packed my suitcase and took a bus into Portland proper. With the few dollars I had, I rented an apartment, bought a newspaper and read the classifieds. The AAA was looking for office help. I walked to their office, spoke to the appropriate people and began filling out a job application. This was my first encounter with a piece of paper that would call for my being less than totally honest. With questions like "Have you ever been in the Military?" and "If so, state type of Discharge" facing me, I knew I had to lie if I was going to get this job. This was also my first realization of what was going to be necessary for me to do if I was going to survive. I lied successfully and got the job.

I had been at AAA for about 2 months when I abruptly decided to quit and move to California. The next morning I walked into the personnel manager's office and resigned. That afternoon I left Portland.

I rented a room in Sacramento and stayed four days. I never looked for a job. I knew I wasn't going to stay there. How I knew this, I don't know. I just knew that Sacramento was too close to what I had just been through. So on the afternoon of the fourth day, I packed my suitcase and walked downtown. I had no idea where I was bound. And I suddenly realized I really didn't care. Whatever happened, happened.

On a spur of the moment decision, I called my sister Irene. She and her husband and family had lived somewhere in Sacramento the past few years, but I couldn't remember where. I'd visit her. I called her at the telephone company. She was surprised but pleased to hear from me, and she picked me up on her way home from work. Once at her home, I knew this also was not a place I could stay for long. It had nothing to do with them. It was me. I had never been at loose ends before and didn't recognize what was happening. I knew I was feeling and acting and reacting as I never had. I know now that my search had begun. I was looking for myself. Irene had always held a certain compassion and understanding for me, and I wondered now if it would help if I told her about my Undesirable Discharge.

I remembered that last December, after deciding to leave the Air Force and being assured I would receive a General Discharge, I had informed my family. After all, I had enlisted for four years and now only two had passed. Some explanation was in order. I wrote two letters: one to my mother who never responded, and one to my sister Bette who responded with: "I know it [the discharge] must be for association because I know you would never stoop to anything that low." And I made one phone call: to my sister Irene. I told her the same story. She asked me if the accusations were true. I sarcastically thanked her for her vote of confidence and the discussion was closed.

It wasn't until seven years later, in 1960, when I was visiting her that the subject of my military discharge arose again. I asked if she had ever considered the possibility that the reason I had been discharged might be true. She looked directly at me and said, "Is it?" I answered with a simple, "yes." She asked no more questions and I was grateful. For the present it was enough that she knew this one truth. Feeling no change in her acceptance of me and reassured of her love for me, I filed away the probability that one day she and I would be able to talk about it at greater length.

After three days I left Irene's and headed for Wisconsin on the bus. Maybe if I went home. . . . I guess home is always a refuge. I knew my mother would not question me, nor would she reject me. Rejection and all its implications suddenly took on a new meaning for me. I felt displaced, with no ties to anyone or any place. I doubted my abilities. For the first time, I was not sure of what I was all about. Maybe going home would give me the answer.

As I expected, my mother asked no questions. She was glad to see me. I'm sure she was lonesome, living alone in Appleton in a small upstairs apartment. She had moved there after my dad died in 1951, and worked every day washing dishes at a hotel downtown. It was a hard job, but my mother had stamina. And it provided her with a way to maintain her independence. She was fiercely independent until the day she died.

With no money, no plans, and little hope, I settled in with my mother. After about two weeks, she asked me if I was going to go back to work at Kimberly-Clark. I had been thinking about that and wondered if I could. I knew that the law required an employer to reinstate an employee who had left to go into military service. I was quite certain this did not include those who had been discharged under other than honorable conditions, but I believed somehow I would be able to get my job back. I had been a good employee and was well liked. Besides, I thought, things couldn't possibly get any worse. How wrong I was!

The following Monday I went to the personnel office at Kimberly-Clark. I spoke to the woman in charge and told her of my previous employment with the company and the reason I had left. She gave me an application to fill out. I sat down with the application and glanced over it. There were the same spaces to be filled in again: "Were you ever in the Military?" and "If so, state type of discharge." I hesitated only a moment. I could not lie on the first one, but I could on the second. And then I could only hope they would not take the time to run a check. So I answered "yes to the first and as I wrote "honorable" in the next blank, I felt my integrity slipping away. I had never bothered very much to assess the makeup of anyone's personality, certainly not mine. But as I felt honesty being replaced with necessity, I wondered if all my values had changed.

I went to work on Wednesday to production control. It was an entirely different kind of work in an office about a mile from where I had worked before. It was good to be back earning a living. There were two women in the office I knew, a few others I remembered from bowling and the rest I made friends with quickly. I took the bus to work for three days and then discovered a woman who lived three blocks from me. After some conversation, she agreed I could ride to and from work with her. Three weeks into my re-employment I decided to buy a car. I had been without my own transportation for almost five months and was beginning to feel the restriction. A fellow in the office was selling his 1948 Jeepster and after seeing it, I knew it was what I wanted. It was a parakeet yellow with a black convertible top that was manually operated and had black side curtains that were easily removed. My first convertible. I loved it! I approached my mother with the idea and she agreed to loan me the down payment. The balance I could finance through

KC Credit Union. This was accomplished within two days. I now had my own car, a good paying job, and a couple of good friends. Things were looking up! It stayed that way for another month.

In the mail, one Saturday morning after I'd been back at KC for only eight weeks, I received a letter from their personnel department. The contents were short –and devastating. They were sorry but they found it necessary to terminate my employment with them. Upon checking, they discovered I had received a discharge other than honorable. Consequently, their obligation to keep me in their employ no longer existed and enclosed was my termination check. I was stunned. Again I had a good work record, had received compliments on a job well done, had been told I was an asset to the office –but was undesirable. They no longer wanted me. I was beginning to believe there must be something wrong with me. But I had no idea WHAT it was. I did know that the home I thought I had found and the career I had wanted with the Air Force ended with their telling me I didn't measure up and now, the first company that had embraced me, rejected me. I cried.

Although my mother asked no questions, I knew she was wondering why I was crying. She sat down at the kitchen table opposite me. For a long time I just cried and she just sat there. Finally, I dried my tears enough to tell her about the letter. I didn't say anything about the discharge, just that I had been fired. My mother was not a demonstrative woman. I don't think it would have occurred to her to put her arms around me and comfort me. Or if it did, I'm sure it wasn't something she was able to do. She said, "You'll find something else." I know that was her way of supporting me. But I didn't feel supported. My whole life was in turmoil; I knew that just giving my best wasn't good enough. I turned it all over in my mind. The fact that I was a lesbian loomed as the biggest obstacle. Everything else, all the qualifications I had, my job performance record, my ability to meet people, my likeability, my willingness to volunteer for any task, my dependability, was meaningless.

My lifestyle was not acceptable to the military. In fact, it was so unacceptable that it overshadowed all else. And that unacceptability, that undesirability, was a matter of record for anyone to see. And it seemed anyone else who saw it would no doubt reach the same conclusion as the Air Force: namely, that homosexuals do not fit in any place, are a security risk and a danger to society, are incapable of satisfactorily performing a job. The best way to handle them was not to employ them or, better still, incarcerate them someplace. I mulled over all this for the remainder of that weekend and the only conclusion I could come to was that as a person, as an individual, as a sensitive human being, as a lesbian, I was worth nothing.

On Monday, after having sequestered myself at home all weekend with my thoughts, I walked downtown to the City Hall. I knew that often there were Help Wanted ads posted there that weren't in the paper or listed with the Unemployment Office. Somehow I felt not having to encounter a person on my way to finding a job would make the job hunting easier. As I scanned the sheet on the City Hall wall, I saw an ad for a typist and general office clerk. It was for one of the small paper mill offices on the opposite end of town from Kimberly Clark. I copied the phone number, called, made an appointment for an interview for the next day and went home.

That night my mind raced with thought of how to handle this next job application I would surely have to complete. It was then I formed the narrative that I would use for the next three decades. I would never tell ANYONE I had been in service. My family would never betray me and Kimberly-Clark was the only employer who had the information. I would never use them as a job reference so no one else would ever know. I would account for my time in service by stating that I had been home taking care of my mother who had been seriously ill. The realization that I was going to use my mother did not sit well with me. I had never thought of myself as a user of people, but I rationalized it away. This was a matter of survival, and up to this point I hadn't been doing very well. I had proof that revealing partial truth resulted in rejection, so I knew full well what the consequences would be if I told the whole truth.

I reflected on my years growing up and how innately I knew that my sexual orientation was not something I could or should discuss with anyone. From the outset it was something I had buried deep within me until I knew the day would come when I would be able to live and love as I desired. I didn't know how far into the future that was; I had no fantasies about it being easy. I just knew that I was a lesbian, I was comfortable with that knowledge and to pretend to be anything else would be doing an injustice to myself. Life had been good to me and I had a strong ego that allowed me to do things other girls my age wouldn't have dared to do. I wore pants all the time while I was growing up. I rode my bicycle fast and furious (like a boy, the neighbors would say). I hitchhiked out to the lake. I danced almost exclusively with girls at school dances and the public dances at the lake. My life had run smoothly; I had the freedom and the ability to make my own decisions and the capacity to handle the consequences of those decisions.

Until now. Now I was looking at the brutal fact that I could no longer handle the consequences of my decision to leave the military service. The undesirability of my character had been handed to me on a piece of paper and reinforced through a letter of termination of employment. I had to face that. I had to cope with that. I had to function in spite of that.

As I completed the job application form at Conroy's Paper Company the next morning, I put into effect the plan I had formulated. I steeled myself against the rush of guilt that seemed to fill my body. I thought of who I could possibly be hurting by my lies. I could think of no one. I repeatedly told myself that I had to work, I had to be self-supporting, I had to take care of myself in the best way that I could. I knew there would never be anyone in my life to support me, and I did not intend to fall prey to extended unemployment and its inevitable outcome. And so the charade began.

Conroy's hired me immediately and within three months I had been given a raise. There was a small sense of satisfaction in knowing I had been successful in keeping my secret and had done my job well. I had never had any reservations about my qualifications in the job market. At times when my skills were lacking, my personality pulled me through. I stayed at Conroy's until the spring of 1955. By that time I had mastered the job, joined the bowling team and learned how to knit.

But I knew no other lesbians in Appleton. My social life was pretty much limited to the weekly bowling and movies. I was dying on the vine. I could have stayed there in the confines of my mother's apartment and the security of my job, but the desire to live my lifestyle and to progress as an individual was strong within me. I didn't know what I wanted to do with my life, except to live it. Surely someplace would find the missing pieces of who I was. I think it was that belief that somehow sustained me for many years.

I left Conroy's in June and prepared to head West in July with Irene and her family when they returned to California from a vacation in Wisconsin. I readied my Jeep, packed my clothes, said goodbye to my mother, and began the trek back to the state where my disintegration had begun.

After two days with Irene in Sacramento, I knew I couldn't stay. That city was in close proximity to McClellan AFB and I couldn't risk running into anyone I had known. So I loaded my Jeep –that wonderful vehicle that somehow gave to part of me a sense of freedom –and took Highway 99 to Southern California.

CHAPTER EIGHT:

PURSUING MYSELF

I drove into Los Angeles, rented an apartment and thought about what I should do next. The next day was Sunday so I drove to the beach. I had no trouble locating the section I was looking for. At Santa Monica Beach in the mid 50's the sand ran all the way up to the highway, parking was no problem, and all along the boardwalk were small hotdog stands and hamburger joints. There were also a variety of gay clubs (one, in particular, where we used to congregate to hear Aggie Dukes play the piano and sing "Grandma Plays the Numbers") and meeting places. I could spend the night on the beach, build a fire, and get up in the morning without being hassled by the police or be disturbed by anyone. Probably the only thing that today remains the same is the friendliness of the gay crowds. I had no trouble making friends. From that day, my life changed. I was swept along on the tide of freedom and liberation.

The group of women I found as soul mates was diverse. There were those who were steadily employed, those who were chronically unemployed, those who were employed off and on, those who were given an allowance by parents who didn't want to be bothered by their lesbian daughters, those who tried drugs, those who did drugs and those who would forever remain clean. Most of these women drank, a few of them didn't, some of them coupled, some were coupled and uncoupled within twenty-four hours, some would never be coupled. Most of them were honest; a few had no values at all. But what they all had in common was the ability to share and a solid sense of loyalty. My friendships with the lesbians in the AF had always been guarded. Each of us was too afraid to show any affection to the other. In this nucleus of women, of which I was now a part, we were never reluctant to give a hug, put an arm around a shoulder or hold a hand. I thrived in all this overt demonstration.

My first move was just off Western Avenue into a two-story white house that nine of these women shared. I got a job at an insurance company on Wilshire Boulevard and began to settle in. Or so I thought. I was operating on a superficial level with everyone, meeting and dating as many women as I could. The incident that ultimately decided for me that it was time to move on was when Nicky (one of the women who shared the house and who was just 18 years old) was arrested and put in the County Jail. She had been picked up on a "morals charge" and was to spend nine days there. I went to see her and the whole "undesirable" record played again. The next day I quit my job, put my few clothes in a box, and moved closer to the beach.

At the beach I met two women who offered to share their small house with me. I moved in there and thought about earning a living. My first job was in a wheel rim manufacturing plant where one of the women worked. I stayed there inspecting wheel rims for three weeks and then quit. That was not what I had in mind for myself. I didn't know exactly what I did have in mind; I only knew there was a part of me that wanted something better, much better.

So I tried the telephone company. Irene had worked for Ma Bell in Wisconsin and transferred to California. She was an exemplary employee, had risen to the management level, and I knew if I used her as a reference, I would be hired. I did just that and was hired as Information Operator. This was during the years when dialing "0" for information meant a real live person would answer.

There were three of us who were going to be the new IO's. We were given a one-day indoctrination into the proper answering technique. Whenever my phone rang, I was to flick the button and answer, "Information." After the caller had given me the name of the number he/she wanted, I was to look it up quickly in the directory. If I couldn't find it right away, I was to get back on the line and say to the caller, "Still checking." If it took me even longer, I was to get back to the caller again and say the same thing. The rule was to never let the caller hang on the line more than 10 seconds without acknowledging that I was "still checking." I had no trouble mastering that technique.

The next day we were put to work. Each Information Operator had a small cubicle by herself (men were not IO's), and I thought my morning went splendidly. I answered all the calls as instructed. Early in the afternoon, my phone rang and I answered most properly, "Information." The caller asked for the name of a person named Ondstradt. I flicked open the directory to the O's and began the search.

More than ten seconds had passed so I went back on the line and said, "Haven't found it yet, but don't go away." The caller said "I won't." Back to the search. I still couldn't find the damn name; I probably wasn't looking for the right spelling.

Back to the line, "That's some name. Give me a clue to the spelling." He spelled it for me. "Right," I said, "I'll find it this time around." And I did. Right there where it should have been between Onbraise and Onnoman.

Back to the line. "I got it, if they haven't moved by now." He laughed. I laughed and said, "You'd better have a pencil handy after all this." I read him the number and then he said, "Nice talking to you" and I replied, "Nice talking to you, too." Nicely done, I thought.

I had just closed the line when I felt the supervisor behind me before I saw her. "Come with me, please," she said. I followed her into the same little room where we had practiced the day before. We sat down. She looked at me first through her glasses and then without them. Then she formed a thin little line with her lips, shook her head, and said disgustedly, "That was no way to talk to a customer. You were given proper instruction in what to say and it is expected that you follow that instruction. Obviously you think you know better. I think it's best you find a different job."

Well! I had tried to take the boredom out of saying the same thing every time to be a little friendly with the customer, and I got fired. I told myself that was okay, though. I wasn't comfortable where I had to sit, anyway. The counter I sat in front of was so low I couldn't get my legs under it without scraping my knees. So it was probably for the best. At least that was my thought as I walked out the building. My next thought was of Irene. By this time in her career with the phone company, she had risen from the ranks of operator to Section Head. This was a major achievement. Now they would inform her that her sister couldn't make it as a simple Information Operator. What would she think? I knew what she would think and I didn't like it.

My mind raced through the years I spent with Irene. She's 15 years older than I am so my memories of her at home are few. I do know that she spent more time with me during my early years than my mother did. She tells me of the times I would jump up on her bed in the morning and scream, "I wanna' say my rhymes, I wanna' say my rhymes," to the point where she was sorry she had ever taught them to me. I have no memory of this, but I do remember how much I loved her and how upset I was the day she came home from Milwaukee where she was working at the telephone company to announce to the family that she was getting married. I went into the bedroom, lay on the bed and cried my heart out. I couldn't believe she was going away. I just knew I would never see her again. She came into the bedroom and lay down beside me. She took me in her arms and talked to me telling me she wasn't going away forever and did I know how much she loved me and that she would always love me. I don't know how long she stayed there holding me, but it was long enough to quiet my fears and end my tears. I visited her a few times after she was married. And periodically over the years I would keep her posted about what was happening in my life. Not much, because it was all during the time I was still in pieces. It wasn't until much later in my adult life that we found each other as friends, as well as sisters. But all the time, her image of me was important.

I knew there was nothing I could do about that then. I drove home and told my friends I had quit the phone company. I couldn't bring myself to tell them I had been fired. Telling them that was akin to saying out loud to myself that I had been given an Undesirable Discharge. I couldn't do it. Numerous times over the past months I had stood in front of the mirror, looked at myself, and tried to verbalize those words. I thought that if I reached the point where I could confront myself with my discharge, I would be on my way to healing. But so far I had been unsuccessful.

I joined a softball team and played Saturday games at the VA Hospital field in Santa Monica, and found a job with a furniture company. It was during my employment with the furniture company that two FBI men came to see me. I was setting up the day's delivery schedule when my boss told me there were two men out front to see me. I panicked immediately. When I saw them dressed in suits, white shirts and ties, I flashed back to the OSI. In a cold sweat I walked up to them. They flashed their badges and asked if they could talk to me. That always struck me as humorous. Asking if they could talk to me. What would happen if I say "no"?

It was the same in the AF. When the phone would ring, the voice would often say, "Will you come to Building 3 please?" I hoped they knew I knew I didn't have an option. I walked across the street with the two agents to a corner take out. We sat down and one of them bought three cups of coffee. They explained why they were there. It seems that while I was in Oregon I had opened a checking account. No problem. Then when I moved to Southern California, I wrote a check on that account and there was no money in it. Writing a bad check that crosses state lines is a federal offense. Problem. I pleaded ignorant. I had forgotten to close that account and, in a hurry, I had written the Oregon check instead of a check on my current California account. They accepted that and as long as it was cleared up within the next few days, there would be no more problem. I quickly assured them it would be and they left.

I felt so vulnerable. It seemed that the government had access to me whenever they wanted. I suppose that's true with everyone. My energies were being consumed more and more with trying to make sense out of my life, attempting to find some stabilizing factor, achieve some measure of worth, and find a clear direction.

I quit my job at the furniture company. Ready for a change of residence, I moved into a house on Riverside Drive in LA with three of the softball players. Once again I went in search of a job. And found one at Gilfillan Bros., a furniture company almost totally dependent on government contracts. By this time my attitude had become one of defiance so when I filled out the job application at Gilfillan, I wrote "yes" under the military service question and "honorable" under the type of discharge question. I was just so tired of lying all the time. This was the best job interview I had had. The working conditions were great and the pay was twice what I had been making. I knew I was taking a chance, but I felt it was worth it and I hoped that maybe they would not run a check on me. I couldn't believe they check every single applicant who came through the door. I passed through two interviews and was hired.

The job was all I expected it to be: challenging, satisfying, stimulating. The fourth day on the job, I was summoned into the Personnel Manager's office. He was abrupt, abrasive, and angry. "This is a government-affiliated company," he said, "and as such every employee is screened for security clearance. You failed the screening. Your application states an honorable discharge from the military service, but the clearance report we received stated you were undesirably discharged and as such are a security risk. Your check is ready for you to pick up now." He got up. I got up. I left the office and without a word to anyone, picked up my check and went home. So much for defiance.

I learned a valuable lesson from that job. The Undesirable Discharge would follow me the rest of my life. It had become necessary for me not only to play the heterosexual games, but to lead the double life most closeted lesbians do. It was also mandatory that I erased from my conscious memory the time I had spent in the service. The government had seen to it that I would pay dearly for admitting to homosexuality. In spite of all that happened, one fact remained clear: I was a lesbian. Of that, there was never a doubt and never regret.

A series of odd jobs followed my short time at Gilfillan. I was still in pursuit of myself. Even though I knew I would never live my life as anything but a lesbian, I knew there was more to me than my sexual orientation. What I didn't know was how to go about finding it. There were gay and lesbian organizations (small and underground) around that I could have turned to for support, but two factors interfered: one was that the women I was associated with were not tuned into (or, I suppose, in need of) organizations, so they were not familiar with them; and the second was that I was not ready to face a group of strangers and tell them about my past. I had not yet been able to face myself with my "undesirability," how could I possibly face others with it? And how could I be sure they wouldn't tell others? I trusted no one.

Then one Saturday night in the late summer of 1956, I met Barb at one of the local Santa Monica bars. At the end of the evening she said to me, "Take me home, Ret." I said, "okay." I didn't know she lived in Massachusetts! However, true to my word, I took her home.

I put my few belongings in a small overnight bag in the back seat of my '48 Jeep and picked up Barb at noon the next day. We were on our way in less than an hour. We had to make this trip in less than a week because one week from that Monday she had to be in class at Westfield State Teachers College.

We drove Route 66, planning to spend the night in Arizona. We got as far as Tucumcarri when the Jeep decided it didn't want to go any further. This was Sunday night, no garages were open, and we had $220 between us. We talked about our options. We couldn't afford to stay there many nights waiting for the car to be repaired. We weren't sure we had enough money to get the car fixed. There was no one we could call to ask for help. We decided to sell the car, if we could find someone on this Sunday night who would buy it. We'd take the Greyhound the rest of the way.

The Jeep sputtered and coughed its way around the hot, quiet town of Tucumcarri until we spotted a fellow working in a salvage yard. I got out of the Jeep, approached the fellow, told him my car had stopped and we had to get to Massachusetts. Would he be interested in buying the Jeep? He came out from behind the fence, walked once around the car and said, "I'll give you a hundred dollars for it." I was ecstatic. Barb was not. She thought we should wait until the garage opened on Monday morning and find out what it would cost to get the car fixed. "Remember," she said, "I don't have a car so when I get to Westfield, we won't have any transportation." This did not seem important at the time. "We'll buy another car," I said. I had already made up my mind.

I hated to part with that Jeep. It was symbolic of so many things: my acceptance at Kimberly Clark (though short lived), my need for independence, my desire to be free (the kind of freedom only a convertible can give). And it was yellow —the shade of yellow that signifies sunshine and sings even on cloudy days. Finally, it was mine (well, mine and the Credit Union's). But I knew it was the only option I had. So I gave the keys to this stranger as he handed me five twenty-dollar bills. Barb and I took our luggage from the back seat and the stranger gave us a ride to the Greyhound station. Three hours later we boarded the bus for Massachusetts.

When we arrived at Barb's home, we propositioned her mom and dad to let us have the front room of the house. It had a separate entrance and although only one room, we could make it into living quarters and it would be private.

They both agreed and it was done. I stayed in Westfield for nearly two years. During that time I worked for a drive-in restaurant as a car-hop (a job that lasted only four hours because I spilled a strawberry malt down the front of a rather buxom lady as I tried to hook the tray onto the car) and then as a short order cook. Even now it amazes me that I was a short order cook. I'm just not very adept in the kitchen. The truth of the matter is that Joe, the manager, liked me so much he wanted me to work there, and since there were only two jobs available (car hop and chef) and I had already bombed at one, he hired me for the other. This was good luck because I took lots of food home. This meant that Barb and I always had enough to eat. I ate most of my meals at the drive-in and made sure I took some kind of meat home to Barb. She was working part-time as a cashier at the local grocery store while going to college so her income wasn't all that great. I stayed at the drive-in for almost a year. Then I applied for a job at Anderson Plate and Metal Company. I filled out the application form using the lies that were becoming easier for me. I could write "no" in the Military Service blank and account for that time lapse by reminding myself that this was a matter of survival. I stifled the voice of my conscience with that reminder. I trusted myself to luck that this company would not make a military check. My luck held and I was hired. I started as a typist and before long I was promoted to Quality Control. I didn't even know what that meant except that it paid more money.

My time in Westfield was satisfying. Barb was the first person to tell me I should think about furthering my education. She felt I was selling myself short by not achieving more and that I would benefit from and respond to mental challenges and stimulation. My job at Anderson's was steady and there had been no problems. We had a circle of friends with whom we socialized and we had purchased a '51 maroon Chevrolet. I was still an incomplete person, but if I didn't think about it too often or too hard, I could ignore that fact and function with the small percentage of me that was still operable.

Then one day in the mail, I received a letter from my mother. It was a short note stapled to a typed letter from the Kimberly Clark Credit Union. The letter stated that they (the credit union) had received notice from the Department of Motor Vehicles that I had sold the 1948 Jeepster registered in my name. Since I did not own this vehicle, and indeed, owed money to them for their loan, I was guilty of a federal offense. (Another one!) The letter further stated that unless the balance of the money owed the credit union was paid within 20 days, a warrant for my arrest would be issued. My mother's note said simply that she had received this letter and had responded by paying the balance of the loan. Her note to me read, "I hope you realize that I do not have this kind of money to spend. I'm trying to support myself and this leaves me with very little money if I should get sick. I hope you appreciate this." She signed it "Love, Mother." As I read her note I felt shame, guilt, unworthiness, irresponsibility, and total despair.

She didn't deserve this kind of treatment from me. She had asked no questions upon my discharge from the service; rather had welcomed me home. She never pried into my business; she carried me financially when my funds were low. And above all: she was not a wealthy woman who could easily afford to pay this debt. I made a silent vow to myself that I would pay back every dollar of the approximate $120.00, which was an enormous sum at that time.

In the early spring of 1958, I packed my clothes, left the car with Barb, and took the train back to Wisconsin and my mother's. The fascination and infatuation Barb and I had for each other had faded and we both knew it was time to move on. We parted the best of friends and although we didn't keep in close contact from then on, my memory of the time with Barb stays vivid and warm. I didn't tell my mother in advance that I was coming; she was taken by surprise. I knew she was pleased to see me and certainly glad for the company. I guess mothers never give up on their children. God knows she had a multitude of reasons to disown me, but instead she hugged me (which was not something my mother did often) and again asked no questions. Why she never asked for any explanations, I don't know. I'm sure she was curious and interested, but she left it entirely up to me whether or not to talk about what had been happening in my life the last few years. I chose not to talk and I knew why. I would have to begin by telling her about my Undesirable Discharge and the severe ramifications that accompanied it. That in itself was too painful. And although I was sure she wouldn't fully understand, I never gave her a chance.

After I had been home about a week, my thoughts again turned to finding a job. In checking the classifieds in the local paper, I saw that Hardware Mutual Insurance Company needed a "raveling" operator. Although I didn't know much about "raveling," I knew it involved typing and I certainly had that skill. I applied for the job using the same technique I had in completing the application form for previous jobs. I held out the hope that not only would they not run a military check on me, but that they wouldn't check my work history. Although Hardware Mutual had an Appleton address, it was not that far from Kimberly Clark. And this was, after all, a small area. My luck held and I was hired. This was a good job, a fun job with people I liked and who liked me. After two months went by, and I still had the job, I figured I was safe. And so I was. I rode the bus to work for the first two weeks. After that my supervisor, who lived a short distance from me, picked me up every day. When I had been there two months, I decided it was time to get my own car and declare my independence again. I bought a 1955 Chevrolet. Not the same as my Jeepster, but then, nothing else in my life was the same as before.

As the months passed, I became more and more aware of my aloneness. I knew it was only a matter of time until my need to be with other lesbians prompted me to make a move. When I approached the Personnel Manager at work about the possibility of transfer to their office in Los Angeles, they were eager to accommodate me. They didn't want to lose "such a good employee." My work evaluations had been impressive and I had begun to feel that maybe I was someone who counted, someone who mattered, someone of value. My self-image had improved; my ego was stronger. I was ready to once again test the waters. And so I moved once again—for the last time--to California.

At first, I was on an emotional high knowing I was in a part of the country where my lifestyle was more acceptable than in the Midwest, but I soon felt fear, a feeling that had been an integral part of my life for so long. I feared I would run into someone I had known in service who would "blow my cover." Or I feared there would be someone at the Hardware Mutual office who would recognize me from the Air Force. Always that heavy dark cloud hung over me. I don't know why I thought a few years out of the Air Force would make a difference. I had begun to put it in the recesses of my mind, and although I could still not face myself and verbalize "Undesirable Discharge," I felt I was coping better.

I settled in Burbank. Two days later on the scheduled date, I went to the Hardware Mutual office in downtown LA. They were expecting me, and all went well until the woman I was to work with took me around the office introducing me. In the field sales office I nodded hello to a woman I knew I had never seen before.

After she said hello, she asked me, "Didn't you work for Kimberly Clark in Neenah?"

A cold paralyzing shot went straight through my body. I felt my heart race and my mouth go dry. With what I hoped was not a change of expression and putting a calm in my voice that I did not feel, I said, "No, but my sister did."

"Oh," she said and smiled at me. There were no further occurrences of this kind; no more were needed. I needed only one of these to alert me to the fact that I was never going to be safe. I was never going to be able to let my guard down. I was never going to be out from under that shadow.

During the year that I stayed at Hardware Mutual I picked up again with the friends I had had before. My life became cyclical: to work, to the bar, to bed, to work, to the bar, to bed. The only changes in that routine occurred when we would head for the beach on the weekends. Many of my friends weren't working, some worked part time, the same old friends doing the same old thing. But they were the only women I knew. And I liked them. Drugs were around and many of these women were users. There were times I was tempted to smoke a joint or get a free sniff of cocaine, but something always stopped me. I knew I had enough problems just trying to get my life back in some order without adding another facet over which I would ultimately have no control. I saw what it did to my friends. I saw what it did to Lynden.

Lynden lived in Pasadena, and I guess I had an ongoing infatuation with her for four or five years. She was cute, talented, personable, but also a hooker and a user. I don't know if I thought I could "save" her, or even if there was anything operating beyond my liking her a lot, but I knew that she was dangerous and that I couldn't get involved with her. I never really knew how she felt about me. One week she wanted to see me all the time, the next she wouldn't talk to me, the next she talked to me only when she needed me. A good friend once told me that I accepted the bad in Lynden and loved what I thought she could be, and that Lynden loved me for all the good life I represented. I don't know if there is any truth to all or even part of that, but I do know that Lynden would often call me in the very early hours of the morning, and in her half-drunken, half-drugged state, ask me to come get her. I never failed to respond, no matter what time it was. She was in and out of jail, sometimes just overnight on prostitution charges, sometimes several weeks on drug charges.

One of the last times Lynden was incarcerated she was at Terminal Island and was given six months. This was the longest period of time she spent in jail, and I visited her as often as I could. At times she would be confident that when she was released, she would stay clean, attend school and start some kind of a career. Other times she would say that kind of thinking was crazy, and that she was what she was and that was all she would ever be. None of her user friends ever visited her at any time she was in jail, but they were always there when she was released. She often said they had a hold on her that she couldn't break. Although I never told her about my time in the Air Force, I certainly could understand what she was talking about in that respect.

The law allowed Lynden to write three letters a month, and I received several while she was at Terminal Island. I know that I saw in Lynden a totally different person from what most people saw. She was an artist. I don't necessarily mean that she had artistic ability (although she did have enough talent that I think she could have made a career out of commercial art). But she had an artist's soul. I knew she was not quick to allow this part of her to be seen, but her letters to me often exposed the essence of her. So meaningful were they to me, that I have saved them all these years.

In August 1961, she wrote: "The Lord's Prayer is playing, the lights have just dimmed another day from my calendar. Now is the quiet time and the only chance I have to gather my thoughts. Constantly I am reminded of the hours and days ticking away, although as though time has forgotten me. I've found myself in a world apart from those that are dear to me. Locks, keys, barred windows and doors have widened the breadth of this feeling. It's almost as though I were drifting along on a tide of undefinable emotion. I'm near yet so far from the something and yet nothing I desire – and never quite knowing causes me considerable heartache."

And in December, one month before her release, she wrote: "Each day is but a day. How very much I've missed your nearness, listening to you –and you, I cannot tell you. I miss you so terribly. I want to see you, be with you, talk to you so much each day I die a little. Never have I wanted to say these things to you –and least of all this way. Part of you is lost to me and has made me sad. 'When Passion turns to ashes, dull and gray, never fan the embers, walk away. Draw the curtain, softly close the door; Remember that I loved you –nothing more.'" Was hers not the soul of an artist? Were those not the words of a poet?

Lynden was released from Terminal Island in January of 1962. In August of that same year, she died at the age of 28 from an overdose of heroin.

I left Hardware Mutual not because it wasn't a good job; it was. And not because I wasn't doing well; I was. I left because I felt like there was no future there for me. I had no idea what kind of future I wanted or even if I had any say in what the future held, but I knew that a typing job at an insurance company was not it. I had been offered a transfer to the Claims Department, which would have been a promotion, but I couldn't deal with the disasters.

From the insurance company, I went to the Unemployment Office looking for a job. I had never had any difficulty getting a job, probably because I always came in first in their applicant typing tests. The Unemployment Office sent me to Revue Studios in North Hollywood. They needed a payroll clerk and I figured I could handle that as well as anyone, even though I had no experience. Lying on the job application form had now become second nature for me. I did it with almost no twinge of conscience. Revue Studios hired me and I began my job in payroll just two days later.

Again, I liked my job. What I liked most about it was that at coffee break and lunchtime we were allowed to go out onto the grounds and visit any of the sets that weren't closed, and the only one that was closed to us was Mark IV, Jack Webb's set.

Consequently, I visited as many as I could and watched the filming of segments of "Alfred Hitchcock Presents," "Leave it to Beaver," and "Wagon Train." I was thoroughly entranced with show business. I should add, though, that finding out how they created "reality" was very disillusioning. During one lunch hour I went on the set of "Wagon Train" and they were filming a chase scene. Ward Bond and Virginia Grey were seated on a buck-board that was bouncing over the prairie being chased by someone or something that wasn't in sight. It was a cruel blow to watch as the buckboard bounced because there was a 2 X 4 under it being pushed up and down by a man at each end. And there wasn't a horse in sight even though Ward Bond kept a tight hold of the reins and yelled, "H'yah, H'yah" at the top of his lungs.

I discovered that working was not the top priority of many of my friends. This being summer, they would spend their days at the beach. Each day it became more difficult for me to get up and go to work, knowing they were sunning themselves.

One morning around 11 o'clock, after almost seven weeks on the job, my phone rang. It was Bobbie, one of my friends.

"Too bad you have to work," she said. "We are on our way to the beach." It was more than I could handle. "Pick me up at noon outside the studio gate," I said. I left Revue Studios that day and never went back.

CHAPTER NINE:

BUSTED

To the best of my memory, my parents had never spoken to me specifically about respect. I mean there was never one moment when either of them told me to respect my elders or the law or each other; but I guess the fact that I did, means that someplace along the line they must have. Certainly during my school years I ordinarily respected the nuns and the teachers, the parents of my friends, older people in general and, of course, the law and the police who enforced the law. I had never been in violation of the law and so it was that I respected the law without fearing it. After my discharge from the Air Force, this was no longer true.

I knew myself well enough to know that I would never flaunt my feelings of disrespect for the law. I would never do anything overt. I wouldn't burglarize or rob or steal; my feelings for the law would manifest themselves in a much more covert manner.

Thus, over a period of slightly more than a year, I had gathered an impressive number of parking tickets. I never bothered to pay any of them and it never occurred to me that the police would care enough to seek and find me. But they did.

Late one Sunday afternoon in December in 1959, there was a knock at my door. I pulled the door open and there stood two "men in blue." My heart stopped.

"Are you Loretta Coller?" the shorter one asked. Actually, "shorter one" is misleading because they were both over 6 feet tall.

I said, "Yes." All the years of lying and faking vanished as I was confronted by the law. My fear of them was not borne out of a healthy respect, but an unhealthy hatred. To me, they represented an authority that was devious and untrustworthy.

They stepped into my house and the second biggest cop said, "We've got a warrant here for your arrest on outstanding parking violations." A warrant for my arrest? Was he kidding? On parking tickets?

"Well, it seems like you have over 60 violations. And unless you have $114.00, you'll have to come with us." I certainly didn't have $114.00 and I didn't know anyone who did. I asked if I could have a day to try to get the money.

"No." I wondered if I could just drive over to a friend's house to see if they had the money.

"No." Could I give them just a kind of down-payment now and the rest later?

"No." They waited until I got a jacket and my toothbrush, and then they escorted me to their squad car. With a cop on each side of me, we walked, and my thoughts went back to McClellan and being escorted off the base. Now here I was between two men again being escorted--this time to jail. For all the miles I had covered, all the lives I had interrupted, all the covering up I had done, I had really made no headway at all.

The cops drove me to Lincoln Heights Jail. There a different cop took my picture, fingerprinted me and booked me. Now I knew I would get a double treatment. Once they checked my fingerprints, they would know I've been in service, why I was discharged, what I'd been doing since, and then only God knew what would happen. The time I spent in jail was unlike anything I'd ever experienced. First I was rudely searched and then marched into a tank (really a big holding room). Here we prisoners stripped, everybody altogether, and were more thoroughly searched and told to get dressed again. Some women were detained, the rest of us were ordered by the matron (a dyke of the 50's who wielded her baton like a phallic symbol) to follow her to a cell. She

103

led us to a large cell that already had about twenty women in it, shoved us through the door, banged the door shut and locked it.

I had been told that as soon as the courts were in session in the morning, a police woman would get me and take me to court. Consequently, when the dyke cop shut the door on us and advised us to get comfortable because we'd probably be there a while, I walked up to the bars and said: "I'm going to court at 8 in the morning, so I won't be here 'a while.'"

I just didn't like her attitude at all. It was after two in the morning, and all I wanted was some sleep. She took one step forward, laid her baton on the cross bar, looked at me, took a step closer, and as her mean eyes narrowed, she whispered: "Whaddaya in for? Get picked up on a morals charge?" And she walked away twirling her phallic symbol. I was so angry I boiled the rest of the night until breakfast time. Then I decided I didn't want to waste any more energy on her.

Breakfast time. God, someone should write a book about that--starting with the melodic tones of the matron yelling, "On your feet, ladies." I don't say it's something everyone should experience, but everyone should at least know what happens.

At 9:30 a.m. a woman officer came for me. She said we would be going to court to answer the warrant charges and that it would probably take the better part of the day because we had to go to three different courthouses. It seems my parking tickets were from three different counties: LA, San Bernardino, and Orange, and they all had to be handled separately. It amazed me as I watched the workings of our justice system. Each court had a file on me that included my personal history. At each court a new public defender would take my file, study it, and plead "guilty." My biggest offense seemed to be that I had been doing all this driving and illegal parking while I had a suspended driver's license. My Wisconsin license was no longer valid; but even if it had not expired, it was the law that every working California resident have a California license.

By 4 p.m. I had been in and out of three courthouses and the total fine due was $155.00. When I could pay this "bail," I would be released. If I didn't have the $114.00 the day before, I surely didn't have the $155 then. I decided to call my friend Phyllis. I was the first lesbian she had met and we had quickly become "soul mates." Our friendship endured despite her mother's objections, her marriage and birth of a son, her divorce, and her affairs with other women. We had seen each other through some hard times and I knew if anyone would have the means to get the money, it would be Phyl.

The police officer loaned me a dime and I made the call. I was right. Phyllis said she would be there within the hour. I had no idea where she was going to get the $155; I knew she didn't just carry that kind of cash around with her. No one I knew did.

At ten minutes after six, the police officer came to the small holding room where I had been since coming back from court, and told me I was free to go. My bail had been paid. I followed her down the corridor past the "community cell" where I had been the night before. The same dyke matron was there, slapping the baton into the palm of her hand. As I walked past her, the sound of the baton hitting her hand seemed to increase. The only joyous moment of my stay in jail happened the next moment. I caught her eyes, held them, and with more intensity than I thought I could muster, I gave her the finger.

It wasn't until months later that I learned Phyllis had taken all the Christmas money she had managed to save and used it to bail me out of jail.

In the summer of 1960, I moved to South Pasadena. I had been between jobs for a couple of weeks and figured it was time to get myself re-employed. I answered a newspaper ad for an office clerk with insurance background. This small office on Figueroa Street was run by one fellow, Matt. His one employee, Ginny, was leaving and I was to replace her. After a short interview and without having to fill out a job application, Matt hired me. I stayed for six months. Then the advantages of a one-girl office were overshadowed by that one disadvantage of being alone all day. Even when Matt was there, which was seldom, he wasn't much company. I quit because I was just too lonesome.

I left South Pasadena and moved to Eagle Rock. I thought about the past years. I realized time had no significance for me. I was 29. I had made little progress from where I was when I stood outside of McClellan AFB seven years before. And I didn't see where it was going to change soon. I realized, too, that accomplishments and goals were not a part of my plan. I had no clear direction in mind and no focus on doing anything specific. Short-term jobs filled my immediate needs. Stability was not important. I felt no need to be reliable or dependable. I had been surviving by my wits and functioning at a level that barely demanded any effort. I wondered what was going to happen to me, why I couldn't seem to get myself all together again and be the person I was, why I had been able to maintain some outside perspective (no drugs, no drinking, no stealing), and yet not be able to see how to fill the void inside. I had no answers. I didn't expect to have any. I was surprised I had the questions.

I continued to pursue myself, moving restlessly around Southern California. Nothing seemed to matter or make a difference; no one was important. I was incapable of trusting, incapable of responsibility; incapable of ending the search for my identity.

I knew that the "Undesirable" tag the government had pinned on me would remain forever like a scarlet letter. My frustration took on new levels with each new day and I wondered how it was all going to end. Would I ever be able to live and function like others? Would I always be "under investigation?" Would there ever come a time when I would not have to lie about my Air Force years? What was I going to do for the rest of my life?

CHAPTER TEN:

BILLIE

In the summer of 1961, I met Billie, and my life took on a whole new meaning.

Even though Billie's life at this point was the antithesis of mine, we found a commonality that allowed us to become friends. From that common bond came a romance that lasted for nine years and a special love that, to this day, endures.

I moved to Ontario and moved in with Billie. I moved from square one to square two. I considered going to college; Billie thought it was a fine idea. I talked about buying a motorcycle; Billie thought it was a ridiculous idea. I registered for college. I didn't get a motorcycle.

Moving to Ontario to begin a life with Billie was a major step. I left behind all the friends I had in the San Fernando Valley; I no longer frequented the bars; I was responsible for my actions. All three of these were total turn-arounds. In addition to that, I entered college, held down three part-time jobs, and shocked my family by having the same return address for longer than five weeks. Most important, I was the recipient of a totally unselfish love that silently demanded I be all I could, and I was the giver of the kind of love I had never before felt.

Living with Billie, loving her and being loved by her was a pivotal point in my life. She had rescued me from myself, saw something worth salvaging, and reinforced every good idea I ever had. It was she who had given me a home, the first in seven years. It was she who rejoiced at my announcement of my intention to begin college at the age of

31. It was she who introduced me to camping and nature. It was she who showed me it was possible to travel for pleasure and not have a need to run from place to place and from job to job.

Billie made her family my family. They embraced me from the outset, literally and figuratively. She set standards and goals for herself, so I began setting standards and goals for myself. She made me believe again that I was worthwhile; I could contribute; I could achieve. She was stable, dependable, compassionate. As a lover, she was faithful and steadfast, giving and undemanding. I wondered if it was too late for me to incorporate those characteristics into my being. From her and because of her, I learned it was not.

But trusting was a long time coming. It was over four years before I told Billie about my military experience. She was the only person in my world who knew the U.S. Government had declared me Undesirable. After the initial conversation, we rarely talked about it. Even though other avenues were opening for me, and I was beginning to experience some small achievements, the wound remained raw and unattended.

My decision to go to college and major in Public Speaking to become a high school teacher, took place during my two years at Mt. San Antonio College. I made this decision with no thought about any impact my Discharge might have. There had not been any occasions for it to be discussed, so I was relatively successful in blocking its reality. I entered Cal State University, Los Angeles, in 1963, and graduated four years later with my intended major. So far, so good.

Then, with the offer of a teaching position, came the application for a teaching credential. Among the plethora of questions asked, the one that jumped out at me was: "Military Service – Yes, No"; followed by "if yes, Type of Discharge." Well, after all those years, there it was again. Now, what?

During this period of time, Billie and I had established a solid friendship with two other women, Dianne and Lou. After some discussion with Billie, I decided to tell our friends about my Discharge and seek their input. Dianne was a teacher and I found comfort in her ability to separate the "honesty" of my application answers from the "truth" of the Discharge. After many hours of deliberation, it was decided I would not tell the truth. I answered "No" to the Military Service question. Then I signed the application on the bottom underneath the statement: "I certify that all the information above is true and correct." With that signature, I created the cloud of fear under which I taught for the next 20 years.

But what were my choices? I saw three. If I told the truth on the application, the issuing of a credential was impossible. No school district was knowingly going to hire a homosexual. I knew the thought processes of the general public and they did not include allowing their children to be exposed to a homosexual teacher. Or I could answer "yes" to the military service question and "honorable" to the type of discharge question. Then I could pray the district would not check my answers. I had been in this situation before and had had to face the belittling consequences of just such a check. My natural instinct for survival did not allow me to even consider this option. Consequently, the only other existing avenue, as I saw it, was to lie.

I knew it was possible that on a given day someone from out of the past could walk on campus, recognize me, and my teaching career was over. I knew this every morning I got up and went to school.

During the years that followed, I enjoyed the friendship and respect of the faculty at the various schools where I taught and the friendship and gratitude of many parents. I resurrected a drama department that had been defunct for several years. To a number of students, this was a lifesaver. It was the prime reason they came to school. The uniqueness of the drama student lends itself to friendships that otherwise would not have existed, and for some, drama gave them their first real friend.

It was my philosophy to put as many students on stage as possible in the two plays we produced each school year. This alone was sufficient to begin making a difference in their ego and self-confidence. They sold tickets with unabashed boldness, saw their pictures in the school paper, and saw their names in the production programs. For me, it was a total team effort. They did everything I asked of them and more. I relished my relationships with these students. My reward was in watching them perform. Backstage after production, parents and friends would crowd into the arena. Flowers and congratulations were plentiful. Hugs were everywhere. The first-time students would introduce me to their parents who thanked me profusely, and those parents I had already met would hug me again. Several parents wrote letters to me thanking me for the difference I made in their child's life.

I often wondered what they would have thought, said, done, if they had known they were hugging a lesbian. There were times when I desperately wanted them to know. I wanted them to know as a statement from all of us. But I knew this was practically impossible.

Still, I built friendships with several of these students who eventually became parents themselves. And it all began with Billie.

PART FOUR:

LOVING AND LOSING
DIANNE, 1970-1984

CHAPTER ELEVEN:

LOVING DIANNE

Over the years that followed, the four of us weathered many crises. Lou's stepfather died; Dianne's dad died; Dianne's mother moved from Donnybook, North Dakota, to Washington for six months and to Dianne's for six months. Billie's mom and dad visited several times.

I graduated from college and we all waited anxiously for the granting of my teaching credential. Those were nervous weeks as we discussed the possibility of rejection. It was certainly within the realm of reality since I had lied on the credential application stating I had not been in military service. When the teaching credential finally came, we all celebrated. That hurdle was over. But continuing to keep the time spent in military service and the Undesirable Discharge from becoming public knowledge would be there for a long time to come. I was subject to dismissal at any time should the truth be discovered.

Dianne and Lou bought a house in Covina; Billie and I bought a house in Irwindale. Lou changed jobs several times and the company Billie worked for changed locations forcing her to find another job. I taught high school English and speech; Dianne taught junior high math and science. There was an affinity between Dianne and me that did not go unnoticed. Often when a phone call needed to be made to Dianne and Lou, Billie would ask me to call and talk to Dianne or when Lou would call and I would answer the phone, she would put Dianne on the phone because we communicated better.

Dianne and I were aware there was something special between us. In the fall of 1965 Billie and Lou decided to take a class at Mt. San Antonio College in Walnut. So every Thursday, Lou would stop by to pick up Billie and go off to school and drop off Dianne who would keep me company. It was during one of these evenings that Dianne and I recognized our attraction for each other. It was as simple as the touch of two hands and the exchange of a look that identified that casual touch as being significant. In silence, we chose to do nothing. The following Thursday, we talked about it. We were both happy in our relationships, had no desire to change anything, and wanted to continue being friends. We put the attraction aside, and from then on, it never interfered with the friendship between the four of us.

Then in 1970, circumstances changed and Dianne and I were again faced with this mutual attraction. In the beginning, Dianne and I thought maybe we should just have an affair. If we could do that and get the attraction over with, we could forget it and settle back into our lives again. And so we met in coffee shops after school and spent hours trying to put our feelings into some perspective. We marveled at our physical attraction for each other; we reveled in the mental stimulation we provided each other. We discovered the commonalties of our values. We became enraptured with each other.

And the more hours we spent together, the more we realized these fragments of time were not going to be sufficient. I knew when I saw the differences in Dianne's eyes as she looked at me that what we thought was a simple attraction was no longer so simple. Her eyes no longer held only the twinkle of new-found excitement; they now were filled with an intensity that seemed to have a life of its own. And from that intensity I saw the love as she held my eyes with hers. I knew that what I saw in her eyes was a reflection of what was in mine.

One afternoon as we were driving nowhere, Dianne reached over and put her hand on the back of my neck. Then she put her face close to mine and said, "Ret, if you don't find a place to park this car right now and kiss me, I'm going to explode." I drove three blocks to the Pomona fairgrounds, pulled in by the grandstand, parked, and kissed her. We shared our amazement at the recognition of the pure physical power of our love.

We knew we had to be very sure of our love and our commitment because there would be no turning back; there would be no bailing out. We were no longer teenagers playing at being in love and moving on. We were two adult women acknowledging our love for each other and within that acknowledgement was the promise of fidelity and the pledge of infinity. We knew it would not be easy; we knew there would be times of turmoil. We also knew we needed to freely express our love for each other and this could not be done as long as I lived with Billie and Dianne had a commitment to Lou. We knew all four lives were going to be touched—and changed. I moved to an apartment and the process of redefining our relationships and restructuring our lives began.

The friendship that existed between Dianne, Lou, Billie and me had been, for all four of us, one worth treasuring. So when the breakup occurred, there were feelings directed toward one another that were foreign to us. Lou felt hate and betrayal; Billie felt abandoned; I felt guilty and Dianne felt healthy. Although she felt a sense of sadness at the end of her partnership with Lou, Dianne was the only one who was able to keep functioning. She was patient as I worked through my feelings of guilt at leaving Billie. I was having an incredibly difficult time. I owed Billie so much. My sense of guilt persisted through the first year Dianne and I lived together. With anyone else, it probably would have destroyed the relationship. With Dianne, it strengthened it. She knew how deeply I loved her and that I was coping with leaving Billie the best way I knew.

Both Billie and I knew that although our relationship had ended, there remained an emotion that was binding. It wasn't just a sense of love; it was more—much more—than that. And because neither of us wanted to forfeit that feeling, we worked intensely for its survival. Billie's dilemma was that she loved Dianne, wanted her friendship, and had no place to vent her hostility and her hurt. And Dianne's love for Billie had not changed. That was clear. Although it was extremely difficult at times, every weekend Dianne and I usually spent one day or part of one day with Billie, from the outset. And though we rarely spoke of it or questioned why, we knew we all still needed each other. Sometimes the awkward or uncomfortable moments were made manageable only through sheer determination and the genuine love that existed. One day, after two months had passed, Dianne asked Billie why she didn't hate her. Billie just said, "I've loved you too many years to start hating you now."

As the months passed into a year, then two, and the three of us continued to spend time together, Billie gradually took charge of her emotions. Although it was a long time before she allowed anyone else into her life, she was slowly willing to admit that she would not keep her heart closed forever.

Now 30 years later, as a friend she is loyal and loving, dependable and resolute. There exists between us a love that neither of us can describe or define. And it isn't necessary for us to do so. The certainty of its existence is sufficient. But it didn't happen overnight; it didn't happen easily; it didn't happen by chance.

With Lou, the breakup took several avenues, all different, all intense, and all of some duration. Her love for Dianne and Billie remained. Her feelings of betrayal by me surfaced immediately. And even though I made several attempts to communicate with her, all channels were shut down. It was impossible to diffuse her belief that I had deceived her. She chose to remove herself geographically from the three of us by moving home to her mother in South Carolina. I regretted her disappearance from our lives; she left behind in me a residue of regret. I thought often of the weekends when none of us had any money and we shared hot dogs with no mustard, how Lou and I were always partners against Billie and Dianne when we played pinochle and of the time we caught them cheating; the camping trips to Kings Canyon.

And I longed for her understanding. But it was not to be. From that distance, sustaining a relationship was difficult; attempting to rebuild one was nearly impossible. And even though Lou corresponded with Billie during this time, it was only long after she returned to California that she and I saw each other.

Dianne and Lou, however, began to build a friendship when she returned. It was mostly through Dianne's phone calls and insistence that they be friends even though her overtures were often rebuked. Dianne worried about Lou and still had a special love for her. Gradually over the years, they came to be able to spend time together; fences were mended between them, and they moved on to a different place in each other's life that was comfortable for them.

Dianne was one of the few people I have known whose childhood was totally happy. For her it was so simple. She loved life on the farm: climbing the windmill and being able to see forever, delighting in raising her pet ducks, finding fulfillment in her rapport with the land.

Dianne's family was a family of few words. Her dad, in particular, was a man who spoke sparingly and made his feelings known through his actions. To him, some things were obvious and didn't need discussion, and some things just were and didn't need any discussion either. Dianne's love for her dad and his for her were obvious whenever they were together. They were cut from the same bolt. Often, when Dianne was in college in Minot and would go home for a weekend, he wouldn't speak to her the entire time she was home. It had nothing to do with his caring or his interest in her, for he would listen intently if she had something to say to him. He just didn't believe in saying words that were said merely for the noise they made

And he was practical. He made do with what he had. One year when they had come to visit, Dianne was sorting clothes to do the laundry. She called for me to come into the laundry room and there we both chuckled at not only her dad's practicality, but at his creativity. She held up a pair of his boxer shorts that he had patched with doilies. It worked for him.

The love between Dianne and her mother was not less deep. Dianne's mother, however, had more of a commitment to the language than her dad and was quick to introduce Dianne to the world of books. Her love of literature began when she was very young and lasted a lifetime.

For instance, Dianne's mother first told me a story that Dianne later would repeat often. One afternoon when she was about two, Dianne's mom was reading to her. Dianne was worried she would never learn how to read because it looked so complicated. She wondered not only HOW she would learn to read, but HOW SOON. Her mother kept trying to reassure her that it would be okay. Then right in the middle of the story her mother was reading to her, Dianne said very seriously: "Oh woe, woe, woe, will I never leawn to wead?" Dianne's mother consoled her, reassuring her she would, indeed, learn to read very soon.

Because of her mother's arthritis and subsequent limited mobility, throughout her childhood Dianne spent a lot of time in the kitchen. She helped and she learned. Both her mother and her Aunt Ruth, her mother's sister, were excellent cooks. And Dianne followed in their shadows. They not only passed on to her the secrets of light, flaky, melt- in-your- mouth pie crusts, but they endowed her with the enviable ability to have all parts of a meal ready simultaneously. She was comfortable and confident in the kitchen.

She was also comfortable and confident in the garage. That is to say, she could paint and hang paper with the best of them. Or install a new electric outlet, or build a solid oak buffet, or restore antique furniture. One time I asked her how she could do all these things so easily and her answer was, "Nobody ever told me I couldn't." It was that simple.

While Dianne was in California and her parents in Donnybrook, she and her mother exchanged letters every week. Often the letters from her mother would be about the garden, what had been planted, the weather and how it was affecting the garden, what they had had for dinner—insignificant things if taken for their face value, but meaningful in their exchange.

Dianne and Dick, her only sibling, also had a deeply-bonded relationship that was rarely expressed in words. Their love for each other was silent and strong.

Dianne was terribly proud of her Swedish heritage. Her roots were deep. She had letters from the 1800's written by ancestors in Minnesota and North Dakota to relatives in Sweden. She had a picture of her great grandfather as a drummer boy in the Civil War. And, although not many of her friends knew it, she was eligible to belong to the DAR. One of her dreams was to visit Sweden and her relatives there.

The farm was as much a part of Dianne as it's possible for an external entity to integrate itself into a person. She was of the land. Sometimes it seemed an extension of her. There was a love and a respect, an appreciation and a wonder, for all things natural. She was curious about our world and the planets surrounding us, as well as the compositions of everything humankind could identify; and so in college she minored in science.

She loved color and texture. She was fascinated with form and balance and dimension. So she also minored in art. Logic, reason, and meaning appealed to Dianne. Precise and absolute in her thinking, the surety of answers satisfied her sense of order. Consequently, she majored in mathematics.

The summer after Dianne graduated from Minot State, she moved to Southern California. She began teaching in a junior high school the following September. One year later our paths crossed for the first time.

My years with Dianne were rich with fulfillment and contentment. This is not to say we didn't have our disagreements and areas of conflict. We were two women whose lives and lifestyles had been totally opposite. That we could come together in any sort of meaningful relationship for any respectable length of time was a phenomenon by itself. That we were able to find a life together so totally satisfying was just short of a miracle.

When I met Dianne she was quiet and reserved. At the time I thought she was rather cold and ungiving. Her behavior and attitude were often mistaken for aloofness. Oh, she was friendly enough when spoken to, but she surely wouldn't go out of her way to make conversation. I didn't think she had much of a sense of humor although she laughed easily enough. As we all spent more and more time together, I saw a different side of her. She was warm and caring, but not demonstrative; she liked to hear a good joke, but rarely told any; she was receptive of others, but not quick to give of herself.

As our years together went by, another dimension of Dianne showed itself. Her sense of humor began to surface and when that combined with her fast thinking, it was a delight.

One Saturday morning, I stayed in bed just a few minutes longer than she. When I got up, she was sitting at the kitchen bar drinking coffee, reading the paper and having a piece of toast. I walked over to her for my morning hug and then went to pour myself a cup of coffee. As I walked back toward her with my coffee, she looked up from the paper and said, "Toast?"

I said, "Yeh, sounds good." Whereupon she lifted her coffee cup in a salute to me and said, "Well, here's to ya."

And she laughed. Really pleased with herself that she pulled that one off. This was barely seven o'clock on a Saturday morning!

Dianne always managed to get her point across. If one method wasn't successful, she had another. I recall one weekday morning when she was in the dressing room getting ready for school. I was in the shower, singing. Now, as you may recall from my Catholic school days, I don't sing well, but that's never bothered me as much as it bothered other people.

On this particular morning I was enjoying the shower, singing "Doe, a deer," and just generally minding my own business. Dianne shouted to me, "Good God, Ret," but I sang undaunted. She shouted at me again and again; I did not respond. So she took it upon herself to get my attention the best way she knew how. Inside the shower stall, just as I sang "Me, a name I call myself," a cup of cold water came from out of nowhere over the top of the shower door and smack down my back.

Dianne was much more homophobic than I. Even she agreed with that. I was always teasing her to do something overt in a public place. Many times when we were riding the escalators in Bullocks store I would lean close to her and say, "Can I have a kiss?" She'd lean back as far as she could without falling off and say, "Ask me later."

Whenever we were in a crowded area, I would casually take her hand in mine and she would just as casually disengage our hands. "We can't do that here, Ret. What if we ran into someone we knew?" I would occasionally answer that with a challenge to her mathematical mind asking the question: "Here we are at the LA Fair, the largest county fair in the U.S.. What are the chances of our running into some heterosexual who could be a threat to us?"

Even if she had no answer, I still couldn't hold her hand. She suffered from that God-awful fear we all know that prohibits us from doing the simple things that bring us pleasure. The things that reaffirm our love. The things that make the public statement of belonging. The things heterosexuals do every day, all the time, any place and take for granted.

So I persisted. Every chance I got I'd take her hand in mine and just as quickly, after a short hard squeeze, she'd drop mine. I figured if I kept at it, she'd see the wisdom of my request. And I was right.

Six of us had tickets to the Greek Theatre on a Saturday evening in July, 1981, to see Anne Murray. We did the whole nine yards: got to the grounds early, spread a blanket, set the individual places, lit a candle, poured the wine, served the chicken, potato salad, and rolls, and listened to soft music from a small radio. It was really quite romantic and Dianne was not adverse to a kiss or two as long as no one was watching.

We cleaned up the area and headed into the theatre. Dianne and I were walking behind two of our friends who were holding hands. I said to Dianne, "Look at Nancy and Jean; they're holding hands. How about it? There's no way, in this whole great big earth, that anyone we know is going to see us."

"Well, alright," she said and slipped her arm through mine and held my hand.

We hadn't taken eight steps before a booming baritone came from behind and said close to my ear, "Well, Loretta, imagine seeing you here at the Greek."

I whipped my head around to the left and stared into the eyes of Wes, one of the math teachers at the same school where I taught.

Recovering quickly, I said, "Oh, yeah, hi Wes. Some night, eh?" Well, I admit it wasn't an impressively intellectual reply, but at least I did get a reply out. Dianne and I quickly reclaimed our own hands and we proceeded into the theatre.

I am the first to admit that when September rolled around and the initial gathering of the teachers was upon us, I had a few anxious moments. However, I had decided before to take the bull by the horns so we would stop thinking about it. I would confront Wes and make it all okay. I didn't have to look far for him. He was right there in the faculty lounge.

I walked up to him and in my most concerned voice, wearing what I hoped was my most concerned expression, said, "Hi, Wes. Hey, ya know that woman I was with when I saw you at the Greek this summer? Well, she's blind, ya know."

Okay, so it wasn't all that great. But somehow I felt I had to explain what he probably never even saw. Such is the power of homophobia.

Dianne and I were closeted. VERY closeted. Some lesbian once said: "I'm so closeted, I can't even find the door." And that was about the category we were in. We had

121

a handful of close friends we saw frequently and who, almost without exception, were not teachers. They were, however, friends of long-standing. Most of them were also closeted. I frequently said Dianne and I could throw a party and have it in a phone booth for all the gay and lesbian friends we had. Because of our limited circulation, there were few opportunities to meet new people. Also, we were teachers, and as such knew the possibility of job jeopardy should our homosexuality ever become known. Although the law states a teacher cannot be fired because of homosexuality, we recognized that our jobs could be made extremely unpleasant. And, of course, we were homophobic. So we were not overtly involved with any gay or lesbian organizations, nor did we participate in any gay or lesbian demonstrations or marches. Until 1979.

That spring we went to the birthday party of a friend. There we met two women, Bunny and June, who became very good friends who were members of (and actively involved in) an organization of lesbians. This organization, Southern California Women for Understanding (SCWU), was based in Los Angeles, and sounded like a fantasy. It was a group of primarily professional women, most of them over 30. Their membership was confidential. Their goals were to establish a safe place for lesbians to share their strengths, concerns, and resources, to find support for their lifestyle, and to eradicate negative stereotypical images of lesbians through example and education.

These goals appealed to us immediately, and we made arrangements to attend the next business meeting. We became members just in time to be a part of their weekend campout in the Malibu hills. This campout was held at an established Boy Scout camp where the buildings were all permanent structures and where there was plenty of space and privacy. We arrived Saturday just before lunch, which was being served in the large recreation room. I had no idea how many women would be there, but when we walked into the recreation room and saw that sea of lesbian faces, I knew there was a heaven on earth and it was located in the Malibu hills.

We became very active in the organization, each of us serving on its Board of Directors. We co-founded a chapter in our own San Gabriel Valley. This organization not only brought innumerable women into our lives, some of whom became very good friends, but it gave us the strength and reinforcement we needed to overcome much of our homophobia. And during that period of my life when the light dimmed and ultimately went out, they were there in astounding numbers offering their love and support.

Few of us are perfectly healthy physical specimens. I am no exception. I don't really have any major problems. The one condition that exists that does cause some concern is my narcolepsy. Briefly, narcolepsy has two primary symptoms. One is excessive daily sleepiness and the other is frequent loss of muscle control. A person with narcolepsy falls asleep at inappropriate times, like in the middle of a conversation, playing cards, or eating a meal.

Dianne, of course, knew almost from the beginning of our friendship that I had narcolepsy. It's not an easy thing to hide. But it wasn't until we were living together that she really had to deal with it. There were times we'd be sitting on the sofa talking and I'd fall asleep right in the middle of a sentence. Sometimes she'd let me sleep; sometimes she'd wake me up. I guess it depended upon the conversation we were having. One time she woke me up and said, "Sweetheart, I don't care if you don't finish telling me the whole story, just finish the sentence." I suppose it did get frustrating.

Sometimes she waited to see what would happen when I fell asleep. For example, we had gone to Riverside to visit Lou and a friend of hers (after we'd reconciled with Lou). The afternoon was warm; Lou had a hot tub. We decided to relax. We were sitting in the tub when I fell asleep—bam, just like that. I had fallen asleep and the top half of my body was ever so slowly falling forward. The three of them were sitting there waiting to see what would happen when my face hit the water. I still can't believe it! Here was the woman I loved having the time of her life waiting for my head to go under water. Thankfully, we are built so that the nose sticks out far enough from the face to be able to act as a warning device.

I believe Dianne and I had one distinct advantage that most lesbian couples do not have: we were friends for eight years before we became lovers. This meant that a lot of things that could have been surprises weren't. The fact that I don't like peas was a mainstay of harassment for years. It seemed that no matter when or where we went out to dinner, the vegetable was always peas. Even when the menu read "mixed vegetables," peas somehow managed to be a part of it. I think with all the other veggies available, someone would be smart enough to take those mothers out of there. Dianne said they were so popular because they were aesthetically pleasing and enhanced the appearance of food. Yeh? So does parsley but they don't put that into mixed veggies.

I know that I'm not a left-brain person. Logical thinking is not one of my big assets. Things that make sense to me that other people say aren't logical and so don't make sense to them. For example, I believe that if I want to put some heat into a room, I turn the thermostat up to its highest point and it will get hot faster. The thermostat acts in the same way as an accelerator. Dianne would laugh. Maybe it's not logical, but every time I've done it, it's worked.

And that part of the left-brain that supposedly functions on those analogy tests did not function for me. Spatial relationships were never my strength. That's why I hate jigsaw puzzles. Every so often over the years, Dianne would buy some jigsaw puzzles at a swap meet or trade puzzles with Billie who also liked to do them. Dianne would set up the card table and begin pouring out the 2,500 pieces from the box. Then she would begin methodically separating them. All the pieces with one straight side would become the border for one edge; the pieces with the opposite straight edge would become the border for another edge. Then she'd separate them by color. Not just distinct reds, blues, yellows, but by shades. This whole preparation technique was more than I could handle. I'd have to leave the room, although it was fascinating to watch this routine. Once in a while after this process was complete and she had taken a break, I'd try my hand at helping to finish the puzzle. I'd sit there for 10 or 15 minutes and not find one piece that fit anywhere. Dianne would come by, stand by the side of the table and look the whole mess over, then casually pick up a piece and, slick as a whistle, just set the damn thing right in. Then, almost without fail, she'd give me a little pat on the back and walk away. I surely didn't need that. I hate peas and jigsaw puzzles.

Being friends for so long also allows you to see each other under all sets of conditions, unlike when you have just met and are dating. Then you put your best foot forward to make the right impressions and often stifle your honest reaction in deference to one that will better impress your date. That gets to be work when you spend a lot of time with just a couple of friends as we did with Dianne and Lou. I finally decided that what you see is what you get. So Dianne knew I was not a good loser. I was not a sore loser; I was just not a good one.

The four of us played a multitude of games (Pinochle, Up the River, Monopoly) and each time I lost or my side lost, I'd moan and groan and carry on, never serious about it. Consequently, one rainy weekend afternoon I suggested we play Scrabble. First mistake. Now, you have to understand my frame of reference here. I have a pretty good working vocabulary, and I didn't anticipate that Dianne would be devious. I had never seen that side of her.

As the game progressed, I was dimly aware that Dianne was considerably ahead of me. I thought I had been doing quite well, forming some pretty long words. And Dianne had been getting short or at least shorter words and yet she was way ahead of me. I finally realized what was going on! She was doing the game mathematically, calculating how much each letter she had was worth and finding the best way to connect it to the letter whose value was highest.

I considered this devious and told her so. It was my understanding that part of the reason to play Scrabble was to increase your vocabulary—not to annihilate your opponent by mathematical deviousness. When I discovered the actual score was 173 to 61, I quit—right on the spot. I quit.

After a piece of apple pie and a cup of coffee, I agreed to try another round. Second mistake. This time I tried to be more aware of the number value, but I lost again, 212 to 104. Then I made the fatal mistake. I said, "Let's play another one but this time don't you try so hard and that will help me to win."

Well! You'd have thought I had asked her to be a hit woman for the Pope. That would be compromising her values; I wouldn't be learning anything; the game would not be honest; whenever she played anything, she played to win. We didn't play Scrabble any more.

For a number of years before we lived together, Dianne knew I was not a cook. I don't mean I was not a gourmet cook, nor do I mean I knew how to cook only certain foods. What I mean is I was not a cook. As much as being in the kitchen was part of Dianne's upbringing, not being in the kitchen was part of mine. My mother never wanted any of us in the kitchen with her. I guess she figured it was more trouble to teach us to cook than it was worth. Both of my sisters got married knowing very little about cooking. So it was natural that I did not have any culinary skills. And throughout my life there never was much reason for me to learn. I was always fortunate enough to be living with someone who did cook and, frankly, I really didn't want to learn.

There were times where I would cook some things. When we were camping, I'd fix pancakes or heat the cinnamon rolls or turn the bacon. And at home I could do a fair job on the grill, but that was pretty much the extent of it. Consequently, whenever I did choose to cook something, either I followed the box directions right down to the comma or Dianne would give me explicit kindergarten directions.

There were times, certainly, during the years we lived together that I did do some cooking. For the most part, they were not highly successful. Dianne constantly encouraged me to keep trying, stating that the law of averages demanded that I have a certain amount of success. Even my stints in the kitchen were subject to her mathematical perception and statistics! For me, the kitchen was a jinx. Two instances that validate my thinking stand out in my memory.

Dianne went shopping one Saturday afternoon in 1978 just before Christmas. I knew she would be gone for a couple of hours so I decided to surprise her by making dessert. We weren't big dessert fans, but there were times when something sweet hit the spot. This seemed to be one of those days. I could have gone right down to Mrs. Simmons' Bakery, but being in the spirit of the holidays, I decided to bake it myself. I knew the limits of my ability so I wasn't about to try anything fancy. I'd settle for just some plain old cupcakes. Dianne always had a box of cake or cookie mix on hand. I found the box of Duncan Hines chocolate cake mix. I read the directions on the back and turned the oven on to "pre-heat" at 350 degrees. I read the directions for mixing the batter. I read each line three times to be sure I wasn't making a mistake. Once the batter was made I tasted it and it tasted like I figured it should. I found the 8 capacity muffin tin, read the directions for putting in the paper cups and followed them religiously. I read the directions for filling each paper cup: "Fill each cup approximately 2/3 full."

At this point I'd like to make it clear that few things upset me as much as being cheated, for example, by bottles of soda that are not filled to the top, or by candy bars that appear longer than they are because a huge piece of cardboard sticks out an inch at each end. Consequently, when I read to fill the paper cups only 2/3 full, my immediate reaction was that in no way did I want a cupcake where the cake wasn't higher than the paper. So to be certain I had a full, rounded cupcake, I filled the papers level with batter. I changed the oven dial from "pre-heat" to "bake," put the cupcakes in the oven, and set the timer for 18 minutes.

Then I remembered when I was little and I would be over at the Saterstrom's when Mrs. Saterstrom was baking bread.

She always told me not to run past the oven or jump in front of it or even open the oven door because this would cause whatever was in the oven to "fall." Well, I believed Mrs. Saterstrom because everything she baked was mouth-watering and never "fell." So I didn't even open the oven door until the timer dinged. But at the sound of the ding I opened the oven door and, wearing a big baking mitt (I DO have some smarts!), I pulled the muffin tin from the oven and set it on a rack. I looked at my creation for a long time. Rather than having 8 nicely rounded chocolate cupcakes, I had a sheet cake with 8 fat legs. The papers were not even visible and the sides of the pan were part of the cake. I didn't know what to do. I wasn't angry; I wasn't sad. I was totally bewildered. I pulled a small piece of cupcake from the pan. Not bad. In fact, it was quite tasty.

I just couldn't figure out how to get the 8 cupcakes out of the pan. After several attempts, I could see it was a waste of time. Not only could I not get the cupcakes out in one piece, I was having a difficult time scraping the cake off the pan. Finally I just threw the whole thing out, pan and all. I poured the remaining batter down the sink and destroyed any remaining evidence. Both Dianne and I believed in honesty. Without honesty there is no trust, and once trust disappears, the relationship is doomed. I don't believe Dianne ever lied to me, and the only times I lied to her were insignificant ones that dealt with birthday presents or surprises or that were answers to the questions "had I seen the box of Duncan Hines chocolate cake mix? Or did I know what happened to the big muffin pan?"

The other example of my kitchen incompetence is one where I am really the innocent party. Dianne and I had been together almost four years when this happened. As we were having our toast and coffee one morning before leaving for school, Dianne reminded me that she would not be coming straight home. There was a math department meeting regarding the incoming 7th graders and she couldn't miss it. So, would I start dinner when I got home so we wouldn't be late?

"No problem," I said. She gave me the scoop. We were having pork chops for dinner. If I would get those started, she would fix the rest of the dinner when she got home.

"No problem," I said.

"Well," she said, "the pork chops are all seasoned. All you have to do is set the oven at 350 and put the pork chops in the oven on the rack. You don't even have to check them because I'll be home in plenty of time to do that." I mentally engraved the important parts on my brain: "350, chops on the rack." No problem.

When I got home from school that afternoon, I immediately went about my assigned task. It was easy since I had the information right up front: "350" – I set the oven dial for 350; "chops on the rack" – I picked up the pork chops and placed them, seasoned side up, on the top rack in the oven. I closed the oven door. No problem. I changed clothes and went outside to do some yard work. About 20 minutes later, Dianne drove up. Her first question was did I put the pork chops on? Of course. No problem.

It seemed like only seconds later that I heard my name being called. I went into the house via the back door that leads directly to the kitchen and could barely see Dianne. She was standing by the oven, holding a plate with two pork chops on it, and surrounded by smoke.

"What's wrong?" My question.

Her answer: "The juice from these pork chops dripped all over the stove and caused all this smoke. You laid them right on the top rack without a pan under them."

Wait a minute here—wait just a minute. My mind clicked into gear and I could hear her saying: "Put the pork chops in the oven on the rack." I had done exactly that.

"You didn't say anything about putting a pan under them."

"Good God, Ret," her very favorite exasperated expression, "you should know at least that much."

Well, I didn't. "I followed your directions exactly as you gave them to me. If you forgot to tell me an important thing to do, I can't see where it's my fault."

She looked at me, then at the chops, back at me and said: "Go back outside. I'll call you when dinner is ready."

"I'll take care of the oven," I said. It's my belief that one of the greatest creations for the kitchen was the self-cleaning oven.

Not only was I of limited ability in the kitchen, but I was also a "picky eater." Those are not my words; they are the words people commonly use to describe my eating habits. I'd rather think of myself as being selective or discriminating or fastidious. The fact is I will not eat anything I cannot recognize, identify or pronounce. And for me, that's a lot of food. I was brought up on roast beef, potatoes, gravy, and sometimes a common vegetable. I can identify all those. Dianne would often slip some exotic vegetable by me by hiding it in something else. She'd cut up pieces of avocado real small and set them in a certain section of the salad bowl. Then at dinner she'd serve my salad and I'd get those damn avocado pieces and not even know it. She did the same thing with mushrooms. Whenever I found one, I'd push it to the side of my plate or eat around it.

Dianne was a really good cook. She rarely fixed anything I did not like. But she prided herself in getting me to eat strange and different things, telling me that it would make meals more pleasurable for me and would give me a better understanding of different nationalities. I already looked forward to my meals and I had no plans for a trip abroad, so it made no sense to me

One afternoon I was out on the front lawn pulling spurge out of the dichondra when she called that dinner was ready. I washed my hands in the garage, came in the house and sat at the bar where we often ate. The napkins and silverware were there along with a glass of wine. No plates. The plates were over by the stove and she was putting dinner on mine. She came back and set my full plate down on the bar in front of me. I looked at it. I had no idea what it was. Whatever it was, it was covered by some kind of sauce. I looked at my dinner.

"What is this?" I asked in my most gentle, curious tone.

"It's dinner," Dianne said, still standing there.

"Well," I said, "I'm not going to eat anything I don't recognize."

She took my full plate away, made a 180-degree turn twice, and put an empty plate down in front of me.

"Here," she said, "Maybe you'll recognize this." Sometimes life is not easy!

Dianne and I saw our relationship become richer and more meaningful. We cherished the time we had together, filling it with picnics, reading aloud to each other, warm days by the pool, walks in the rain, intimate conversations, and political disagreements—the free and simple things in life. We enjoyed season tickets to the Ahmanson Theatre, weekends in San Diego and Sea World, air balloon rides, a vacation to Nome, Alaska, where Dianne stuck her foot in the Bering Sea, camping across Canada and in the rainforest of Washington, sightseeing the New England states. It was an added blessing that we were both teachers and could have the summers together.

We knew how fortunate we were to have each other; we took nothing for granted. We appreciated our friends and

 enjoyed socializing. We contributed our energy, time, and funds to lesbian causes. We worked to enhance our teaching skills. We supported our favorite charities. We voted at each election. We continued to grow as individuals and as a couple. And most of all, we relished our days and nights together and reveled in our love for each other. As true romantics, we believed our life together would never end.

CHAPTER TWELVE:

LOSING DIANNE

The summer of 1982 was no different from any other summer—except that it was the beginning of the end for Dianne. Only we didn't know it.

It was June, the afternoons were hot, and we were spending our leisure hours by the pool. One Saturday, after being outside for a couple of hours, we came into the house for a noon snack. Sitting at the bar, wrapped only in our towels, which by now had fallen to our waists, I looked at Dianne's back to see how much sun she had gotten. The mole between her shoulder blades looked different and I mentioned this to her. "How does it look?" she asked me. I tried to describe it to her. It was still a brown mole but it looked like there was a black dot in the middle of it. Just a very small black dot, about the size of a dull pencil tip. It was so small and I REALLY wasn't sure it hadn't always looked like that. We both forgot about it until the following week, lying nude on our stomachs on the patio reading, I glanced at the mole again. This time it DID look different.

I said, "That mole looks like the black dot has gotten larger."

"Are you sure?" Dianne asked.

"No, but I'm going to draw a picture of it and then we'll look at it again in a few days and see if there's any change."

I did just that. I tore a small piece of paper off a note pad, took a pencil and drew what I thought was an accurate picture of the mole. I even labeled the black dot so I would be sure to have a correct representation for the next time I

132

made a comparison of the mole. I realized that I couldn't commit to memory what the mole looked like and be certain my memory was true. Drawing the picture would at least trigger my recall. I put the paper in the drawer and forgot all about it. We both did. Our minds were on our upcoming vacation.

Visiting the New England states in the fall, when the leaves are most brilliant, had long been one of the things on our "wish list." We knew it was an impossibility since school was always in session at that time, but it was still something we talked about. In May, we had decided this was the summer we would vacation on the East Coast. Planning this vacation was no small task. Making the plane reservations was the easiest part. Locating Bed and Breakfast Inns and corresponding with them either by mail or by phone was more difficult and time consuming. We had to have a working time frame from which we could make our reservations. Our estimated driving times and lengths of stay in different places changed almost every time we worked on the plan. In addition, there were all the mundane things that everyone has to do before leaving on vacation: arranging for care of the dogs and the house, payment of bills and picking up of the mail, notifying the police of our absence, canceling delivery of the newspaper, to name a few.

Even though both Dianne and I knew the slight change we observed in the mole was important, we became engrossed in our upcoming vacation, the ending of the school year, and all the everyday happenings—to the exclusion of giving any more attention to that mole. On June 14, Dianne had what she referred to as "an attack on her right hand." Her wrist and fingers were swollen to the point where that hand was practically useless. This was her strong hand, and having that immobilized was frightening for her. She saw it as a severe arthritis attack, called our physician and received a cortisone shot. This relieved the pain and the next day her hand was fine.

In June, we flew to Boston, rented a car, and began our bed and breakfast inn tour of the East Coast. We were gone a month. It was thoroughly enjoyable--a week longer than most of the summer vacations we took. When we returned from our vacation in mid-July, we picked up our life where we had left it: spending leisure time by the pool, being involved with SCWU, attending the Ahmanson Theatre, and socializing with our friends.

A few days after our return, Dianne had a severe attack that this time involved her right hip. It happened suddenly, without warning. She could not walk from the family room to the bedroom. I half dragged, half-carried her and put her into bed. The following morning there was no trace that anything had happened.

Sitting by the pool one afternoon in early September, I suddenly remembered the mole. I told Dianne to bend forward and let me look at it. Now the mole looked REALLY different. There was what appeared to be a white mark along one side and the color of the mole seemed to be darker than before. I went into the house, scrounged through the desk drawer and found the sketch I had made in June. Comparing it to what the mole looked like now, there was a definite difference. "You'd better see a doctor about that, just to make sure it's okay." I knew changes in moles were a danger signal the Cancer Society warned about. Dianne said she'd call the doctor for an appointment later that month.

Still, there was no worry, no urgency—from either of us. We felt so secure. Cancer happens to someone else. Our main focus was Dianne's arthritis, which didn't seem to be getting any relief from the current medication. The mole was secondary.

When Dianne returned from her September 16 visit to our physician, she said she'd forgotten to ask her about the mole. Neither of us viewed it as critical. During her October 18 appointment, the mole did come up, and our doctor suggested that it should be examined by a dermatologist. She referred Dianne and Dianne made an appointment for October 28.

At that appointment the dermatologist removed the mole and told Dianne he would send it to the lab for biopsy. We waited for a call from him with the results. When after a week we had heard nothing from him, Dianne called his office. The nurse told her on the phone that the mole had been diagnosed as malignant. They then set an appointment for Dianne to see the doctor again on the following Monday, November 8.

I was not at home when Dianne called the dermatologist's office. I was teaching drama and the fall play was two weeks from opening. We were in the final stages of rehearsal that took place every evening after school and that lasted all day Saturday. I didn't get home until 10:00 PM. When Dianne told me about her conversation with the doctor's nurse, I couldn't believe it. I have never heard of a nurse giving a diagnosis of cancer to a patient over the phone. I cannot begin to describe the intensity of my anger at both the doctor and his nurse. I asked Dianne what kind of cancer it was, but she didn't know. The nurse had just casually dropped the bombshell that it was malignant. We were stunned. We talked about cancer generally and, although we were intelligent enough to recognize this as serious, I think both of us believed the worst was over.

Dianne wanted me to go with her to her November 8 appointment with the dermatologist, but she didn't want me to go into the doctor's office with her. I didn't know why, but whatever her reasons were, I respected them without question. When she came out of his office, she said that the pathology report was "malignant melanoma." The doctor was certain he had removed the entire growth, but to be sure, she should see a surgeon and have him excise the area. Neither of us had had any contact with a surgeon for several years. So, when we got home, we went through the Physicians and Surgeons yellow pages of the telephone book until I recognized a name. Dianne made an appointment to see the surgeon on November 18.

Opening night of the fall play was November 17, 1982. I was there that evening in body only. My mind and my total emotional being were concentrated on Dianne's appointment the next afternoon. The strength that we gathered to face this crisis came from each other. Only a few very close friends were aware of Dianne's diagnosis. We saw it as a temporary condition.

When we went for the appointment, there were two other people in the waiting room. Dianne and I approached the receptionist and confirmed her appointment. The woman on duty asked Dianne what it concerned. Dianne's voice quivered only a moment when she told her, "I had a mole removed that was diagnosed as a melanoma and that doctor said I should have a surgeon excise the area." The minute the receptionist got this information she was out of her chair and in search of Dr. Vanderhoof.

Dianne looked at me and smiled, "Boy, when they find out you have cancer, they really move!"

We didn't even have time to sit down before the nurse appeared and told Dianne the doctor "will see her now." Again she went in alone. When she reappeared, she looked relieved. She held out a yellow paper that reflected the procedure just done, the diagnosis, and the charges. I looked only at the first two: "Lesion previously diagnosed as malignant melanoma—wider excision: 6 cm x 2.5 cm skin surface area excised – Diag: No residual melanoma. Return."

I looked at Dianne, still smiling, her eyes no longer showing fear, and I felt a smile start at the tips of my toes and work its way all through my body.

"That's it?" I tried to form the words though my smile.

"Yep," Dianne said jauntily, "I have to come back in three months for a check. 'Routine,' he said. And I have to come back on December 1 to have these stitches out. Other than that, that's it!" I hugged her right there in the office, in front of the receptionist and the two people who were still waiting. We stopped to celebrate on the way home. She had a Big Mac and a vanilla shake; I had a Quarter Pounder and a strawberry shake. We each had a large order of French fries.

The stitches were removed on December 1 and Dianne and I celebrated the coming of 1983 like two troopers who had just won the war. Dianne made her scheduled three-month visit to the surgeon on April 20 and again was told there was no evidence of recurrence of the cancer.

During this time, Dianne began talking about finding some other form of relief from her arthritis pain. The medication she was getting no longer seemed to be effective. I was never aware of the severity of her pain because she never said anything. Only when it became almost unbearable would she say something. Now it seemed lately the pain had been pretty constant with only minimal relief. And so she consulted with Dr. Tong and on June 24, Dianne had her first gold shot. The following Saturday we went to the bookstore and bought a Physician's Desk Reference so we would know the side effects of the gold shots and, consequently, be on alert for them.

On the evening of Wednesday, July 13, Dianne had pain in her right hip. As the evening progressed, so did the pain. If she remembered the incident with this same hip a year before, she didn't say so. It never entered my mind. Later when we did talk about it, we wondered if the pain the year before was related to the pain this night. She went to bed early hoping that lying down would relieve the pressure or whatever was causing the pain. It didn't.

At 4 AM she got up to go to the bathroom and couldn't step on her right leg. I had been partially awake all night, conscious of her movements, so when she sat up on the edge of the bed and then attempted to get on her feet, I was wide awake. I went over to her side of the bed and sat down beside her. Agony was in her eyes. It hurt just to sit there. She put her arm around my neck, and I helped her as she hopped to the bathroom. When she was back in bed and the pain was still intense, we talked about going to the emergency room at the hospital. She said she'd really rather wait until Dr. Tong was in her office to see if she could get in to see her. I reminded her that was several hours away, but she thought she'd be able to tolerate the pain until then.

At 6 AM Dianne changed her mind and agreed to go to the hospital. I put my Levi's over my shorty pajamas, pulled a sweatshirt on and slipped into my Birkenstocks in less than

30 seconds. Dianne sat up on the edge of the bed again and I put a lightweight jacket around her shoulders. She put her arm around my neck and stood up. She hopped about ten feet and then said she couldn't go any farther; it just hurt too much. For a moment I didn't know what I was going to do. I knew I couldn't carry her. How was I going to get her out to the car?

It took only a moment before I had the answer. I told her to lean against the doorway between the bathroom and our bedroom and that I'd be right back. I went out to the garage and took the old green dolly down from the hook. I figured I could set Dianne on the dolly and wheel her out to the car. But I needed something to set on the dolly for Dianne to sit on. I decided on the three-foot tall orange stool. The legs were about two inches square at the bottom and I decided that with two of the legs on the dolly it would be strong enough to support her. I raced back into the house with the dolly in one hand and the stool in the other. In spite of the pain Dianne managed a smile when she saw what I had.

"Is this going to work?" she asked.

"I hope so," I said, as I leaned the dolly back toward me and set the stool on the dolly at the same angle. It fit. I pushed it over to where Dianne was leaning and said, "Okay, sweetheart, sit on the stool and when you're ready, I'll tilt it back just enough so I can push you out to the garage."

She hopped to the stool and sat down. Even that hurt. I eased back on the dolly, saw that the stool wasn't going to slip and pushed her through the house, into the garage, and up to the car door. I helped her into the car and we were on our way.

The hospital is normally about a twenty-minute ride from the house, but I'm certain it didn't take me that long to get there. I pulled the car up to the wheelchair ramp, ran into the hospital, briefly explained Dianne's condition, grabbed a wheelchair, and went back out to get Dianne. The Goddess was watching out for us because there was no one ahead of us in the emergency area. A nurse wheeled Dianne into the treatment room and I followed right behind. She helped her get up on the gurney and from that position got all the paperwork completed. The doctor was there almost immediately and I was asked to leave. Within ten minutes the nurse came out and told me I could go back with Dianne if I wanted. I walked back in and Dianne was in the same condition as when I left her. She said they had called Dr. Tong and weren't going to do anything until she got there.

Dr. Tong arrived within the hour and immediately hospitalized Dianne. She went through a series of tests. I was so worried and scared. I wondered if it had something to do with the gold shots and I wondered if Dr. Tong knew what she was doing even though Dianne had full confidence in her. Dr. Tong had ordered Dianne's hip to be put in traction and had varied the poundage until Dianne stated the weight was tolerable. Dr. Tong had also ordered physical therapy for Dianne every four hours

Each day Dianne was in the hospital I surprised her by showing up at 6:30 AM with coffee and the newspaper. Sharing those two things every morning during the summer was one of the luxuries we allowed ourselves. During the school year it was limited to the coffee, but during the summer months there was time to read the paper, too. She asked me how I got in because visiting hours didn't begin until later and the front door was locked. I told her I came in the same way we had the morning before, through the emergency entrance. Dianne so thoroughly enjoyed being able to read the paper first thing in the morning that I decided there was no reason why we should have to alter our ritual. Dianne stayed in the hospital over the weekend and I brought her home on Monday since her hip had returned to normal. There was no residual pain nor was there ever a recurrence of that attack.

Dianne saw the surgeon on July 21. His diagnosis: "No evidence of recurrence of cancer at this time. Return." With this piece of news we were even more joyful. Surely now there was no more danger. It had been eight months since the mole had been removed. Dianne had, for all practical purposes, been given a clean bill of health.

For Christmas that year, I gave Dianne a heavy-duty dolly I had bought on sale at Ace Hardware. I figured if we had to do the "pain-in-the-right-hip-emergency trip" again, we'd be ready to do it in style.

Dianne looked good, she felt healthy, and we both had peace of mind. As far as we were concerned, the bad time was over. Like many others, we had found the cancer in time and had been successful in winning the battle. We no longer thought about it. It would stay that way for only four more months.

In early January of 1984, we decided this was the year to have an anniversary party. It would be 13 years sometime in February (we could never decide on a date so we usually just celebrated the whole month) and we hadn't really had a full-blown party since 1981. Dianne and I decided to go against tradition and flaunt our disregard for superstition by celebrating our 13 years with a party. We chose the 25th of February.

The wisest move we made for that anniversary party was to videotape it. A good friend had a video camera and she asked if we'd like her to film it. We'd never done anything like that and it sounded like a great idea. The day of the party the filming went from sedate pictures of women in casual conversations to "on-the-spot" interviews. It couldn't have been better if it had been planned. There are some portions more precious than others: Dianne being interviewed, the two of us dancing on the patio, the bedroom where we laid on the bed and proved to them we still remembered how to kiss. What a treasure I have in that videotape!

Easter vacation that year was the third week in April. We had decided to spend the week around the house doing the multitude of work inside and out that homeowners must do. Early Wednesday morning, April 18, Dianne was standing in front of the dressing room mirror wearing only underwear. I was getting dressed. I watched her move from that mirror to the larger one on the bathroom door. She was looking at her left upper arm and shoulder. She called me over.

"Look at these two spots, honey."

140

I looked where she was pointing. There was one small purplish black spot on the outside of her arm near her shoulder and another one on the backside of her shoulder. They were about the size of pencil lead. I was surprised she had even seen them. I rubbed my finger over them; there was no raise in the skin.

"They don't look like moles," I said. "Did you just notice them now?"

"Yeh," she said, "I was looking to see how that scar on my back was healing and I saw them. I guess I'd better call the doctor and have him check them."

I agreed. "They're probably nothing, but it's a good idea."

Neither of us mentioned cancer. They were merely two dots that had never been there before. I had been getting little red dots on my body lately. Red dots that eventually turned brown and became what I guess are liver spots. So the appearance of these spots on Dianne didn't impress me as all that important. And from her reaction, they didn't seem that important to her, either. Later that same morning, Dianne called the doctor and the earliest appointment she could get was for the following Monday, the 23rd.

Once again, I was in dress rehearsal for a play, so when we talked about whether or not Dianne wanted me to go to the doctor with her, her response was, "What for?" Indeed, I thought, 'what for?' So, when Dianne went for her appointment she was alone. I stayed at school and supervised the dress rehearsal.

When I got home that night around 9 o'clock, she was sitting on the couch reading. We talked about how dress rehearsal had gone and about her visit to the doctor. She said he had looked at the spots and removed them. He would send them to pathology and let her know the results. She showed me the two small incisions he had made. Both just had band-aids over them. She was to return Wednesday, May 2, to have the stitches removed.

The spring musical opened on Wednesday, April 25. Dianne was planning to attend the next night. She really was supportive with my productions. More often than not she would build the set or at least the most difficult parts, and she always gave me explicit directions for the parts she didn't build.

After Friday night's performance, when I arrived home around 11:30 Dianne was waiting up for me, watching TV. We talked about how the play went, how her day was, just generally relaxed, and then called it a night.

We had only been in bed a few moments when Dianne said, "We've got trouble right here in River City. The doctor called with the report from the pathology. Both the spots were melanomas."

My mind went blank. What did she say? Melanomas? Where did they suddenly come from?

"What?" I asked. "They're melanomas?"

"Both of them," Dianne said.

My mind couldn't seem to grasp what she was saying. Both melanomas? What did that mean? Dianne said no more. I raised up and leaned on my elbow. I looked at her and for the first time in almost two years, I saw fear.

"Did he say anything else?" I asked.

"No, just that he would see me Monday for removal of the stitches."

My mind raced. I knew Dianne was healthy. We had stopped smoking in 1975, and although we didn't play any vigorous sports, we did walk regularly and we maintained a good diet. In all the tests she had ever had, her heart was strong, lungs clear, and blood pressure good. She never even had any cavities. The only problem had always been the arthritis.

"Well," I said, "Those spots were awfully small. As long as he cleanly removed them, there shouldn't be anything to worry about."

I believed that. She looked at me with an expression of hope and trust and agreed I was probably right. I lay back down, put my arms around her and held her close to me. It took a long time for both of us to fall asleep that night.

Late Sunday afternoon, April 29, we decided to take a shower together and get to bed early. As we stood in the shower, Dianne noticed another spot on her left arm.

"Is this what I think it is?" she asked.

I looked at it through the shower water. "It looks like it is," I said.

We just looked at each other, finished showering and stepped into the dressing room to towel. She moved closer to the mirror and looked at that spot, turned halfway around, lowered her shoulder and said, "Is that one?" I looked at the new spot, then looked at her. It did look the same. Where were all these spots coming from? Were these melanomas, too? They were all so tiny. This made four of them. I put my arms around her without saying anything. I just held her close and we stood like that in the dressing room for a long time.

On Wednesday, May 2, we both went to Dr. Vanderhoof. She didn't want me to go in with her so I sat in the waiting room. When she came out, she motioned for me to come with her. As I walked with her back into the doctor's office, she said, "I asked the doctor to remove those two spots we found. He feels pretty sure they are melanomas. He said he wanted to talk further to me but I told him I wanted you to be there."

He was sitting behind his desk when we walked in. He invited us to sit; we chose to stand. He said, "I think you should see a cancer specialist. Dr. Kempf is at Norris Hospital and Cancer Research Center. He is a most respected oncologist. If you like, I'll call him now."

An oncologist? Cancer Research Center? Where was that? My mind reeled.

Dianne asked, "Does this mean that the cancer has entered the bloodstream?"

"Yes," the doctor said, "we believe it has."

There was just the slightest change of expression in Dianne's face. I thought, cancer in the bloodstream? How did she think to ask that question? And what did that mean? God, I suddenly realized how little I knew about the body. I

143

had a pretty accurate idea of where the major organs were located and what their functions were, but I never even understood the bottom number of the blood pressure test. I put my arm around Dianne and we looked at each other.

"Shall I call Dr. Kempf?"

"Yes, please," Dianne answered.

We stood and waited while he placed the call. When Dr. Kempf was on the line, the doctor handed the phone to Dianne. She identified herself and spoke briefly, then hung up. She looked at me and said in a voice that was almost steady, "I have an appointment for next Friday." I nodded. We left the doctor's office and drove home.

She sat close to me on the way home, her hand resting on my leg. We both were trying to draw strength from the other. We said little. I seemed to be frozen in this moment in time, and Dianne was gone somewhere in her own thoughts.

When we got home, we sat on the couch and held each other. Soon the tears came. We talked quietly about what this new discovery meant. Dianne said she was sure she'd have to have some kind of treatment. I agreed.

She said, "Well, we won't know exactly what kind of treatment, but whatever it is, I want to get started with it now and get it over with."

I was sure we were on top of the whole thing because we had done exactly as the doctors had suggested. Besides, she looked so healthy. She hadn't lost any weight and she was lightly tanned from the sun. And except for the arthritis, she felt good. I said as much. She looked at me and just slowly nodded her head up and down. Tears came to my eyes again. I felt that awful hurt in my throat, the hurt I was going to feel so often in the future. We tried to make some sense out of all this. There was none to be made.

The tears were rolling down my cheeks and Dianne was crying softly. Then as the tears subsided, she said, "You know, Ret, the only way we're going to make it through this is with the help of our friends." She was right; I agreed with her. We could support each other and share our strength, but we were going to need more than that. We were going to need the support of our friends. That meant we would have to tell them. They couldn't help us if they didn't know. And we could not pretend everything was wonderful when our world was falling apart. She decided she would tell our friends as the opportunities to do so arose.

Around 6 o'clock that evening the phone rang. I answered it. It was Flo. The minute I heard her voice, I began to cry. She asked what was wrong. I told her briefly what the doctor had said. I heard her reaction—stunned silence. She said she'd call back. I had no sooner hung up the phone when it rang again. This time it was Jan. We went through the same short questions and answers. Then she hung up. I don't believe 45 minutes had passed before the front door bell rang. There stood Jan and Flo and Coe.

There was a sense of love and friendship and support and compassion that evening such as I had never felt before at any time in my life. Dianne and I needed some guidance and assurance that our decision to tell our friends and thus gain added strength was the right one. By the time the three of them left around 10 o'clock, a special bond had been formed. They had shared with us the beginning moments of a crucial and critical time in our lives. We had bared our very souls to each other, and in that process had been fused together in a special way. Throughout Dianne's illness, those three women would prove to be Gibraltars for both Dianne and me.

We each called school the next morning and told them we wouldn't be in the next two days, Thursday and Friday. It was all so overwhelming. We needed time with each other, and time alone, to try to comprehend the incomprehensible.

Dianne wanted to drive to Laguna Beach on Thursday. Normally, given her choice between a woodsy area and the beach, she would have chosen a woodsy area. But this was not a normal time and today she wanted to be a part of the endlessness and timelessness of the sea. We had lunch at one of the outdoor cafés, and talked of small things; the many sea gulls landing so close to us, the smell of the fresh salt air mixed with the heavy smell of foods frying, the overweight waitress in too short shorts. We walked the water's edge for a long distance and sat, in silence, on a rocky edifice that epitomized the strength and tenacity we needed. The sun was hot even with the chilly sea breeze. It was a strangely comforting time. Conversation was sporadic. Dianne commented, as she had done on happier times in years past, on the endlessness of the sea, its timelessness and its capacity for devouring and for cleansing. Each of us needed to come to terms with what had been said and what had been determined as fact. I knew that Dianne was digesting what little information we had and attempting to put it into some framework she could understand and cope with. After about an hour, she was ready to go home. Whatever it was that she had been looking for or hoping to get from the sea, she apparently had gained. There was a sense of quiet about her that had not been there earlier.

"I have to call Dick," she said, referring to her brother.

"Yes," I agreed, "are you going to do that tonight?"

"I guess so," was her soft answer.

I knew it was a call she dreaded making, and there was no way I could make it easier for her. She dialed Dick's number and after a few preliminaries, she said, "The cancer has returned with a vengeance." She had revealed her perception of her illness.

The phone began ringing early in the evening; the network was underway. It seemed more difficult to deal with other people's shock and fear and hurt than it was to deal with our own. Dianne didn't want to talk to very many people, so I answered all the calls. It was exhausting just to keep telling the same facts over and over again. Yet there was no way I could not do this. Each woman calling had the right to know and, more importantly, we wanted her to know. Nevertheless, it was draining. I knew, though, that the feeling was miniscule when compared to what Dianne was going through.

We had made plans for the upcoming weekend. Friday night I was scheduled to do a Special Interest Program (SIP) for the Ventura Chapter of SCWU, and Saturday and Sunday we had planned a camping trip to Lake Casitas with Dee, Susan, Flo, Coe and four other women.

Friday morning we packed the car and were on our way to Ventura before noon. We talked about my giving the SIP that evening and I told Dianne I wasn't sure I'd be able to do it. It was a parody and as such was filled with humor. My heart was heavy; I didn't feel very humorous or light-hearted and besides, much of the humor seemed dependent upon Dianne being with me.

Lou was at home in Oxnard when we got there. We were planning to stay the night and this was the first time Dianne had seen Lou since the melanomas had been diagnosed. So, after the unimportant preliminaries everyone goes through, our conversation turned to Dianne's health and what had transpired up until now and speculations about "what next?" I knew Dianne and Lou had to have some time alone together to talk about the cancer. I also knew that a special love existed between the two of them of which I was not a part and that it was important they have private time to express this love. Since we were leaving early Saturday morning for Lake Casitas, the only opportunity they would have would be that evening.

I felt I had an obligation to do the scheduled SIP. Oh, I suppose I could have called the Chair of the Ventura Chapter and told her about Dianne and that under those circumstances there was no way I could follow through, but then what would all those women do who had planned to come hear me speak? I felt I had to appear. I did not expect Dianne to go with me; I knew she was not up to any emotional upheavals right now. We talked it over and agreed I should go. If I didn't feel as though I could do the planned program, I shouldn't. If I wanted to tell the group about her, Dianne said that was okay. If I just wanted to make a brief appearance and then come home, that was okay, too. Dianne assured me I would be sensitive enough to the group to know what action to take. And she was right.

When I arrived at the Savings & Loan Building where the SIP was to be held, there was a crowd of 45-50 women. I

147

was pretty impressed. Right then I was glad I had decided to go.

As it turned out, I did not give the scheduled program. When we had all assembled, I simply told the truth as best I could. I told them Dianne had just been diagnosed as having cancer; I told them about the melanomas; I told them about the surgeries; I told them about Dr. Kempf and the Norris Hospital and Center for Cancer Research; and I told them how bewildered we were and how much we were going to need their support. I told them all these things as my eyes filled with tears and the tears rolled down my cheeks and the lump in my throat kept getting bigger making it harder and harder for me to talk.

Dianne was very well-liked and the women reacted to this news about her with sympathy, compassion, and support. Many of them cried with me. I left knowing there was a tremendous amount of love encircling us, and an unlimited number of shoulders to lean on.

We were up early Saturday morning, and after Lou cooked a Southern breakfast of black-eyed peas and grits, Dianne and I were ready to leave for Lake Casitas. I put our small suitcase in the car. We said our good-byes. I felt sadness because Lou wasn't coming with us, and was planning to move away again, this time to the East coast. I liked her and I would miss her.

Dianne had a very hard time saying goodbye to Lou. They both cried. Dianne had the feeling she would never see Lou again. As we drove to the Lake, Dianne's tears continued. She was certain this was the last time she would ever see her former partner. I couldn't understand where this idea came from. Who had told her such an idiotic thing? Why did she believe this? No one had even intimated such a happening, I told her. I told her to stop thinking those thoughts and focus on a couple of years down the line when we would take a trip to the East and visit with Lou.

"Don't even think about such things until at least you've had a chance to talk to Dr. Kempf," I said.

"It's just a feeling I have," she said.

After awhile her tears stopped. She leaned back in the seat and, exhausted, fell asleep.

As the week began and each day brought us closer to Friday, May 11, when we would see Dr. Kempf, we tried to keep our routine normal and our thoughts on the tasks at hand. We both went to school each day fulfilling our responsibilities. I was resentful of these mornings when I would have to leave Dianne to spend the time elsewhere. We were anxious to see the doctor just so we could get some answers to our questions. Dianne was eager to find out specifically what was happening to her body and what was going to be done about it.

"It's the God-awful not knowing that's tying me in knots," she said one evening. "I imagine all sorts of things. I'll sure be glad when Friday's here and we see Dr. Kempf. Then at last I'll know something. Whatever it is, it's better knowing than not knowing."

Our appointment with Dr. Kempf was for 10:00 AM. We were there by 9:45. We parked the car and as we walked up to the hospital entrance, we looked up at the name: The Kenneth R. Norris Jr. Cancer Hospital and Research Center. "Well," Dianne said, "they put it right out there, don't they?"

We went to the Information and Appointment Counter and Dianne told the fellow who she was and he confirmed the appointment. We sat down in the large waiting area and talked in low tones about the people we saw coming and going. Many of the people were in pairs and at one point Dianne said, "Gosh, with some of these couples coming in, it's hard to tell which one is the cancer patient. They both look so healthy." And she was right.

"Well," I said, "it's no different from us sitting here. If someone were to look at us and try to decide who was the patient, they'd have a hard time because you look as healthy as I do."

"That's true," she said, "then there are those who are obviously the patient, like that woman over there."

I looked in the direction she nodded and saw a woman who looked to be about Dianne's age standing by the information window with a younger woman who was probably her daughter. The older woman had only half a face. It looked like she had had several surgeries that had taken most of her nose away and had left only a small portion of her mouth. Her neck had a huge indentation on the same side. I looked back at Dianne and I knew what she was thinking. She was silent for about five minutes. Then she looked at me, and angry, frustrated and confused, said, "Ret, what the fuck am I doing here?" She rarely used such language. And then she took my hand.

By 10:30 we still had not been called for our appointment. It's never easy waiting to see a doctor, but this wait seemed to be forever. I walked over to the fellow at the counter and asked him if he knew how much longer it would be. He really didn't know. Dr. Kempf had been delayed at UCLA and the word was he would be here shortly. The wait was taking its toll on both of us, making us more anxious as the minutes ticked by. First we read magazines. Then we read all the plaques on the walls. Then we read the unbelievably long list of donors and patrons. Finally we looked in the window of the closed gift shop. Everything served only as a short-term diversion. There was no dismissing or ignoring the reason we were here.

Finally at 11:15 a male nurse came over to us, asked which one of us was Dianne Anderson (positive proof of how healthy she looked) and said for us to follow him. We walked down the corridor in silence. He led us to a small room, told us to make ourselves comfortable and that Dr. Kempf would be there momentarily. Dianne and I sat down on two of the three straight chairs that faced the small desk.

"Well, now at least we'll get some information on what's going on," I said.

"I just want to get started on whatever it is I have to do. Not doing anything about it is driving me crazy." Dianne looked around. "Look at this room, will you? What do you suppose they use it for? It's barely big enough for one bed."

She was so angry. She hadn't lashed out at anyone; at least not that I knew about. But she was so enraged that as desperately as she tried to control her anger, periodically it would surface. Most often it was directed at objects or situations or conditions, such as now with this room. I was acutely aware that in all the conversations we had about this awful discovery, she never questioned aloud, "Why me?"

Within ten minutes, Dr. Kempf appeared. He was a small man, by most standards, white hair (not gray), glasses, and he filled the small room with confidence the moment he entered. He apologized for being late and asked which one of us was Dianne (again reinforcing our idea of how healthy she looked). When Dianne acknowledged him, he shook her hand. She introduced me to him as "Loretta, the woman I live with." He shook my hand. This was the first time either of us had ever had a consultation of such a serious nature with a doctor and we really didn't know what to expect.

Dr. Kempf carried two manila folders with him, which he laid on the desk as he sat down.

"Give me a few minutes to go over the files and re-familiarize myself with the details," he said as he picked up the first folder. He methodically went through all the papers in the folder re-checking each item with Dianne.

When this was finished he closed the folders, looked first at Dianne and then at me and asked, "Do you both want this to be an honest conversation?"

Without hesitation, we both answered "yes." We had already talked about this aspect of it and knew we wanted to have the truth so we would know what we were really dealing with. Dr. Kempf was wonderful. He was clinical, patient, thorough, truthful, compassionate, and guardedly optimistic. He remained that way throughout all our dealings with him.

He gave us some information about melanomas, theoretical and factual, including the fact that they have one of the lowest survival rates – 30%. His treatment suggestion was resection of locally symptomatic lesions and then following Dianne closely at monthly intervals. (His medical notes reflect his hesitancy to put Dianne on toxic chemotherapy because it gives little likelihood of major regression with negligible response rates.)

He told us that the major problem with melanomas is that by the time the mole looks different enough to be concerned about it, it's usually too late. When Dr. Kempf said "it's usually too late" Dianne and I looked at each other. Then Dianne turned her look to Dr. Kempf and asked, "Are you saying my cancer is terminal?"

"Yes."

I knew this was not happening in real life. I knew this was some sort of nightmarish fantasy Dianne and I were playing out, and soon this scene would fade and be replaced by the reality of our love and our life as it really was.

"Do you have any idea of how much time we're talking about?" Dianne wanted to know.

That's a strange question, I thought. Time for what? Then it occurred to me she was asking about length of treatment. But Dr. Kempf hadn't suggested any specific immediate treatment. So that wasn't the thrust of her question. Time to live? Number of mornings left to get out of bed? Number of days left to be together? Number of months remaining of our life together? Number of years left to accomplish all we had talked about when we thought we had an abundance of time? I brought myself back into the soft dialogue between Dianne and Dr. Kempf.

"My guess would be anywhere from six months to a year and a half," was Dr. Kempf's gentle answer.

My mind jumped to the best case immediately: we had eighteen months left to be together. Is that what he just said? How was that possible?

"I'd like to get started on whatever treatment you have in mind," Dianne said. True to her word, she wanted to be "doing something" about this disease, and thereby have a modicum of control, rather than let the disease proceed as it pleased.

Dr. Kempf said he thought a bone scan was in order and would schedule her for one as soon as possible. In the meantime, he suggested Dianne should consider attending group therapy in an effort to learn how to deal with her cancer. He looked at me and suggested it might be a good idea if I were to join a similar, but not the same group. We both agreed that was a good idea.

We had no more questions; Dr. Kempf had no more information. At 12:40 we walked out of the hospital. The nightmare was real.

Dianne had decided she would not keep the facts of the disease a secret. Although she would not inappropriately blurt out her recent diagnosis, she would not hesitate to reveal it if she were asked or an opportune moment for its disclosure presented itself. Most of our friends and the staff at her school already knew about the melanomas. What only a few of them knew was the time element Dr. Kempf had recently indicated. Now, she told me, as soon as she learned the results of the bone scan, she would make all that public knowledge, too. In the meantime it was her desire to "live our life the same as we always had." So we went to Bunny and June's for dinner, spent time with Billie and Ellie, saw Jan frequently, met Flo and Coe for dinner, and proceeded to do the things we had already planned.

Recently we had been discussing what Dianne wanted to do on her birthday. She would be 45 on May 18. For the past several years, Billie and Ellie had celebrated their birthdays with us. The four of us would go to a relatively nice restaurant chosen by the celebrant, and after dinner return to one of the two homes for cake and coffee. We had long ago ceased giving gifts and were quite satisfied with this arrangement. Occasionally another person or two would be invited along, but we kept the number small. Dianne's birthday was approaching and she still had not decided what she wanted to do. We hadn't talked about it now for several days, but I felt she would bring it up when she was ready.

Monday morning as we were getting ready for work, Dianne suddenly stopped combing her hair, looked at me and softly said, "You know, Ret, I could die tomorrow and it would be okay. I don't want to, but it would be alright because my life has been full and content." My eyes met hers and for that moment our love was tangible, concrete, absolute.

Later that day, May 14, Dr. Kempf called and told Dianne the bone scan had been scheduled for Thursday the 17th at UCLA. We were both eager to have the scan done since we believed it would give us more in-depth data about the status of the cancer.

I arranged to take Thursday off work and together we drove to Westwood. While Dianne was having the scan, I busied myself with grading papers, taking short walks, watching people, and worrying—not necessarily in that order. By mid-afternoon we were back on the freeway headed for home. During that drive she talked about her birthday.

"I think I want my birthday dinner to be just the two of us, Ret. I don't feel like I want to socialize much."

"Okay. That's fine. Where would you like to go?"

"No." She changed her mind. "I can't do that to Billie and Ellie. The four of us will go out as we always have."

I assured her it would be okay either way.

"Or maybe we could have just a small group," she went on.

I told her I thought that was a good idea, too. We could invite six or eight friends we liked to spend time with.

"No," she said, "I don't want a group. I don't want it to look like it's my last birthday and have everybody feeling sorry for me."

I kept quiet. I had never seen her so indecisive about anything. Finally she said, "How about the four of us going to El Encanto for dinner? And let's ask Marty, too."

I waited only long enough to see if she was going to change her mind again. When she didn't, I answered. "That sounds good. I'll call them when we get home tonight and then I'll call the restaurant for a reservation."

We followed those plans exactly, and for all intents and purposes it was like any other birthday dinner. Dianne was determined it would not be a sad evening and it wasn't. I watched her as she set the tone for the evening, my love and admiration for her growing. Next year, I vowed silently to myself, we would do something extra special for her birthday.

With Memorial Day weekend fast approaching, we made plans to have a few friends over for a cook out. Dianne had not deviated from her initial statement to keep on living as we had been. But before we could enjoy the weekend, there was one more trip to be made to the surgeon. He was scheduled to remove three melanomas on Thursday, the 24th. These short surgeries were beginning to take an effect on Dianne's endurance. Dr. Kempf had suggested previously that if more melanomas appeared, she should not have them removed, but she could not tolerate looking at them.

As we walked from the doctor's office to the car, Dianne said, "He had a real hard time stopping the bleeding today. He had to press on two of the areas a long time before the blood clotted."

That fact didn't strike a cord of concern in me. There were times when I had cut myself and it took longer to stop the bleeding than other times.

"Did he say anything about that?"

"No."

"Well, if it was something to worry about, don't you think he would have said something?"

"Well. . . maybe."

"I'm sure he would have. He's been real up front with us."

It wasn't until the following Sunday when Dianne was putting on her bathing suit that we saw an indication of how hard the doctor had had to press to stop the bleeding. The spot on the front of her right shoulder had been red on Thursday and today was terribly bruised as was the incision on the left side of her back. They were so bruised, in fact, that Dianne said she wasn't going to wear her bathing suit or any other top that didn't cover those bruises and the rest of the incisions that were still obvious. She just didn't want everyone to see them. That led to our discussion about friends and not having to hide anything from them. I finally convinced her that these women coming today were more than friends. They were women who truly loved her. If she couldn't be herself, if she couldn't feel comfortable in not having to hide from them something as simple as a bruise, if she couldn't allow them to be a part of the entire ongoing process here, then she was only kidding herself and me when she repeatedly said we needed our friends to support us through this. She agreed and spent the rest of the day in her bathing suit.

This was a rough day for Dianne. Her back was terribly sore and she didn't move much. She rose to the occasion, however, as always, and played checkers and bridge most of the afternoon. We never imagined the day was a prelude to the coming week, which was filled with nights of pain, shots and pills, and frustration. Throughout them, my heart ached. There was nothing I could do to make her comfortable and I would have done ANYthing.

On Monday, Dianne didn't even try to get out of bed and she didn't mention school. This, by itself, told me how awful she felt. Every other time when she stayed home, she would talk about the ramifications of her not being at school. Now, when she didn't even mention it, I knew she was really hurting. The intensity of the pain was obvious every time she tried to move or turn over. Still she complained very little; the telltale signs came from her involuntary moaning and grimacing.

On Thursday, May 30--two weeks before the end of classes, I put things in order with a substitute teacher—just in case. I resented having to leave Dianne to go to school, but I had a responsibility there that I couldn't ignore. And if there was one thing I had learned from Dianne, it was to fulfill my responsibilities. If she knew I had stayed home without first putting things in order at school, she would be furious—and disappointed. My thoughts were focused totally on Dianne and my desire to get home to her as soon as possible, yet I fully planned on being back in school to finish out the year. I knew how Dianne hurt now, but I also knew that as soon as she could see the doctor, she would be feeling better. Of this I had no doubt. Once I made arrangements at the school, I was home to Dianne by noon.

Dianne was still in bed when I got home, with intense pain in her back. She had gotten out of bed once to go to the bathroom. No easy task. I told her I thought I should call Dr. Kempf. She reminded me he had told us he would not be at his office or at the hospital. He had a doctor covering for him, and we could call that doctor who was knowledgeable about Dianne's condition.

"Okay," I said, "I'll call whoever it is that's taking his place." I remembered Dr. Kempf had said a woman doctor was covering for him, but that if Dianne needed him, we should call. The message would be relayed to him and he would call us. I reminded Dianne of this.

"Well, let's wait a little longer," she said. "I'll try to eat something so I can take another pill. Maybe that will at least help me sleep."

There were times when I could disagree with Dianne on an issue and ultimately convince her to see it my way. There were other times when I disagreed with her and at those times she would show me the illogical thinking that led me to my opinion, and I would be convinced to see things her way. There were other times when I could disagree with her and there was no meeting of the minds. In those cases we just accepted the fact that we disagreed and respected each other's opinions. And then there were the times when she had made up her mind about something. When that was the case, there was no moving her from that conclusion. This, I learned, was because she had thought it all through, weighing all possibilities pro and con, before coming to her decision. The majority of the times, however, were governed by how important the issue was to the other person. If it was extremely important to me and not to her, she acquiesced and vice-versa.

I tried to assess the situation now. I didn't want to argue with her about calling the doctor; she had some strong feelings concerning her health and her control over it. On the other hand, I felt we needed to find out what was happening with her body, why her back seemed to be under attack, and get her some relief from the pain. I decided to try to make a deal with her.

"Okay, sweetheart," I said, "we'll try another codeine pill. But if you don't sleep or the pain doesn't subside in a couple of hours, I'm going to call the doctor."

She agreed. She sat up, took another pill and lay back down. I sat on the edge of the bed and held her hand. I felt her forehead and cheek. She didn't feel exceptionally warm, but I wondered if she had a fever. I had taken her temperature several times over the last week and it was always normal or very close to it. She closed her eyes and after several minutes of watching her, I got up and went to the living room.

I made a couple of trips back to the bedroom checking on Dianne. As long as she had her eyes closed and was lying still, I didn't disturb her. At 3:45 PM when I made a trek to the bedroom to check on her, she was awake and obviously in extreme pain.

Dianne fought the intensity of the pain until 11 PM when I finally persuaded her that it was all right to call Dr. Kempf. He said to call in an emergency, and I defined this moment as an emergency. I was frustrated with my inability to do anything to relieve Dianne's terrible agony. One of the promises I had previously made to her was that she would have no more pain than was necessary for diagnostic purposes, and that I would never allow her to be in extended pain. I intended to keep that promise for both of us.

I placed a call to Dr. Kempf and there was no answer at the hospital number he had given us. I hung up and immediately called the emergency room number of Norris Hospital. The female voice answering the telephone took my message and said she would have Dr. Pinterbrown, the doctor on call taking Dr. Kempf's messages, call me. I waited a stressful 45 minutes and when the phone didn't ring, I placed another call. This time I asserted myself, becoming rather aggressive and stressed the fact that Dianne was a private patient of Dr. Kempf's, and that she needed immediate attention. I'm certain I was less than cordial, but at that moment I really didn't care. The woman I loved was in the other room in more pain than I ever want to see anyone in again, and she was depending on me to do something to alleviate or at least relieve that pain, and I couldn't even get anyone to return my calls. Jesus God! It's so awful not to have some kind of influence or clout. If we had been famous or noteworthy, action would have been taken immediately. God—I was mad!

The phone rang – finally – at 12:10 AM. It was Dr. Kempf. I explained Dianne's condition and he asked about her urine, bowels, temperature, appetite.

"The best thing for you to do is go to the hospital. I'll meet you there, in the main lobby, in 45 minutes," he said.

I told Dianne and she was in such anguish she did not protest. My mind was swiftly turning over ways I could get her to the car. My thoughts fleetingly turned to the dolly I had given her for Christmas and the stupid note tied to it. I had done that in jest, never for a moment even considering the possibility that it would come to be true. And now it had, but I knew the dolly was not the answer tonight. The pain was too terrible for Dianne to sit on a stool and be subjected to that makeshift traveling. She'd have to walk.

I backed the car out of the garage and turned it around so the passenger door was on the house side. At least that would help a little.

I went back into the bedroom and helped Dianne sit up on the edge of the bed. I put her bedroom slippers on her feet and slipped a jacket over her shoulders. The nights were cool even though it was June and I didn't want to take any chances on her getting chilled. I stood in front of her and with my hands under her arms, I pulled her to her feet. She clenched her teeth, but didn't say a word. She put her arms around my neck and just stood there for a moment. I held her close, trying to absorb some of her pain.

"Ok, honey," she said, "let's go—slow." I thought the walk to the car would never end. To Dianne it must have seemed like forever.

I drove to the hospital as fast as I dared. Just as we entered the gates, Dianne said, "I'm sick. You'd better stop the car." I pulled over to the curb and before I could move toward her, she had opened the door and was vomiting in the street.

Dr. Kempf was waiting for us in the lobby. He took one look at Dianne, put her in a wheelchair and as we followed behind, ordered one of the male nurses to take her to an examination room on the third floor. There he quizzed Dianne about the same things he had asked me earlier. In addition, he questioned her about the area of pain. Then he called for anther male nurse to wheel Dianne to the second floor for x-ray. I couldn't go along; I had to wait where I was. My mind was trying to make some sense out of all this. I wondered what had happened. I couldn't make a connection between melanomas and the kind of back pain Dianne was having. But there had to be a connection. I took solace in the fact that Dr. Kempf was a respected oncologist who really seemed to care about Dianne. I knew the best of everything was available to her here at Norris: physicians, facility, staff, equipment, and knowledge. My head was filled with questions: What was he going to do about Dianne's pain? Would she have to stay here now? What was the best thing I could do to help her? How bad was this? What was he examining her for? I hoped he would remember the pain she was in when he examined her because I knew Dianne would not tell him. Finally around 3:30 AM they returned. Dianne had been given x-rays and a CAT scan. Dr. Kempf said he would call us tomorrow with the results and depending upon what they were, he and Dianne would set up a specific treatment schedule beginning on Monday, June 4. For now, he had given her a "pain shot" and it seemed to be working.

As we left the hospital at 3:45 AM Friday morning, June 1, I put my arm around her and we walked to the car in silence. The pain shot seemed to have accomplished two things: it had caused the pain to subside, and it had made her sleepy enough to doze all the way home. It was almost five o'clock by the time I helped Dianne get into bed and crawled in beside her. She lay on her right side; I lay on my left side. We just looked at each other for several minutes. Then I asked her if the pain had subsided any, and she said it had, enough to be able to sleep.

"Come lay by me," I said as I opened my arms. She raised her head off the sheet and moved toward me. I looked at her and glanced at the sheet. There was a small wet spot where a tear had fallen. She looked at me with those beautiful blue eyes that now were filling with tears and asked, "What if I don't get better?"

"You will. I know it. Deep in my heart, I know it."

I believed that. Oh, sure, I knew there was some time element involved, but that was eighteen months away. For now, I knew she would feel better as soon as Dr. Kempf started her on a treatment program. I knew the summer months would be good ones; they always were and I was looking forward to them.

"We'll just take it one day at a time. You know what you always say, 'I'm not afraid of tomorrow, for I have seen yesterday and I love today.'" I held her close and felt her body relax just a little. I tried to swallow around the hurt in my throat.

At 6:45 AM, I got up. The doctor had given Dianne a prescription for pain pills and I wanted to get that filled as quickly as possible. As soon as I got home with the pain pills, I gave her one glass of apple juice. She had no appetite and I couldn't convince her to eat anything. Following the directions for use on the pill bottle, I gave her another one four hours later. Between the time I had given her the first pill and four o'clock, when Kathy and Mary arrived, Dianne had vomited three times. She had called me twice to help her to the bathroom because she was nauseous. She knelt on the floor by the toilet bowl, and I knelt beside her with my left hand on her forehead and my right arm around her shoulders. This enabled me to support her head and hold her close to me. She hadn't eaten anything so she had no solids in her stomach. Both times her nausea culminated in spitting up clear liquids and having a severe case of dry heaves. The third time she was nauseous she called me, but told me she didn't think she could get out of bed. I brought the basin in from the bathroom, and from a slightly elevated position, she went through the same thing yet again.

Shortly after Kathy and Mary arrived around 4 PM, Dianne was still sick. I told them how often she had vomited throughout the day and that I thought maybe I should call the doctor. This nausea was something new. I didn't like it; it scared me. And it was very hard on Dianne. I knew Dr. Kempf would not be in his office or at the hospital this entire weekend, but he had left with us the name of the doctor who was covering for him. At six o'clock I called the doctor and was told he would call back. At 6:45 he did. I identified myself, and he immediately told me he was familiar with Dianne's history. I was impressed. I told him about Dianne's nausea and he said he'd call our pharmacy with an anti-nausea prescription. The pharmacist called a few minutes later to say the prescription was ready. Kathy picked it up, and when she returned home and gave it to me, she said the pharmacist told her the pain pills Dianne was taking should be taken only with food. This was the first I had heard that and I was angry. Because I did not know that, she had had to go through all this nausea. I opened the anti-nausea prescription and was surprised to find a box of suppositories. I told Dianne what the pharmacist had said about eating and the pain pill. She just looked at me. Then I said, "I'm not going to give you the 10:30 pain pill unless you eat something."

"What?" was all she replied.

"I don't know. I'll find something simple and easy."

She smiled. It was her first in many days. Then I told her what I had for her and she smiled again. God, it was great to see. She said that seemed like a strange prescription for nausea, and it certainly seemed odd to plug that end. I agreed. But I did it, and eventually it gave her some relief from the nausea. At that time, I thought she might eat something. I asked her and she agreed she would try. She managed to get through one-half piece of toast and almost a full cup of hot tea. This was the first food she had eaten since Thursday.

Dianne's lack of appetite was apparent. She was eating as a means to an end. She never talked about the degree or intensity of her pain, but we struck a bargain: ¼ bowl of cereal plus a small glass of apple juice equaled a pain pill. Just because we repeated that pattern frequently didn't make it easy. Once or twice she got up and sat in the chaise lounge on the patio to read the paper. I viewed these occasions as unexpected progress. I knew Dianne had strength she hadn't yet revealed to anyone.

On Saturday, Ellie was due to come over around noon to remove the stitches from the latest melanoma surgeries. Dianne thought she would sit up and wait for her, but after about twenty minutes she decided to take a shower. She declined my help so I stood by as she readied herself. I sat on the toilet seat cover while she was in the shower. I knew she would function by herself as long as she could; only when she felt herself past the point of no return would she ask me for help. It had nothing to do with love; it had nothing to do with need. What it had to do with, I am sure, is the estimation of the essence of which she was made. Her mother, even in her wheelchair, rarely hoisted the flag for help, and her dad, in his short illness, never had the opportunity to do so. Consequently, there was no way she was going to signal unless defeat was apparent.

She managed to get showered and her hair shampooed before asking, "Ret, honey, are you there?" I answered her and she said she didn't feel good.

"I can't find the 'off' handle." She was momentarily disoriented.

I slid open the shower door, reached into the shower and pushed on the handle until the water stopped flowing. She was standing with head bowed and both palms pressed against the shower wall.

"I don't know, Ret, I don't think I can do this. I feel sick."

With all of my body in my throat, I grabbed the bath towel, wrapped it around her, wet hair and all, and half carried her to bed. I sat on the edge of the bed and gently towel-dried her hair. After about fifteen minutes, she felt better and quietly fell asleep. Later, when Ellie arrived to remove the stitches, Dianne made no attempt to get out of bed.

Throughout the day we bargained, and each time I threatened to withhold the pain pill unless she ate something. I told myself that what would have been cruel under any other circumstances was now kindness. I told myself that and yet every three to four hours when she insisted she just couldn't eat anything, I had a difficult time making her earn her pill.

As the day passed, I thought about Monday when I would have to return to school leaving Dianne alone. I did not intend to stay the entire day at school, but there were records I needed to drop off in order for final grades to be issued. I knew Dianne couldn't be by herself. The only person I knew who had the time to give and with whom I could entrust her care was my sister, Irene, who lived in Sacramento. I called her, briefly summing up the last two days and then asked her if she could come. She paused only long enough to ask her husband Mark what time they could leave on Sunday morning.

Mark and Irene arrived early afternoon. After Irene visited a short while with Dianne, who was in bed, we settled in the living room. Around four o'clock Dianne slowly walked into the room. She sat in the swivel chair; I put her feet up on the hassock. As she maneuvered to get comfortable, the bottom part of her right leg was uncovered. She stopped all activity, looked at her leg and pointed to a spot five or six inches above her ankle.

"Is that another one?" Her voice was so small.

I just glanced at it. It looked like the others.

"I think so."

She looked straight into my eyes and I would have done anything, committed any crime, denied myself everything, if

I could have changed what I read in her eyes. Instead I did what I could; I put my arms around her and held her.

Dianne was asleep the next morning as I dressed and readied to leave for school. I left the bedside not telling her I would be home as soon as I could.

Irene was in the kitchen drinking a cup of coffee. I told her to call me if anything changed. She promised she would, and I drove to school grateful, once again, not just for Irene being here, but grateful that I had come out to her so many years before. Had she not known of my lifestyle and my relationship with Dianne, so much would be different. I would not have been able to make the decisions regarding Dianne's treatment that I had without Irene wondering why Dick did not have input. I would have been at a loss to explain the countless women now concerned and calling, and later, continuously in attendance. It would have been difficult for me to give logical reasoning for our joint financial holdings that would be tapped. And most important of all, I would have had to stay guarded in my feeling for Dianne, careful not to be too concerned or too loving. And now more than ever I needed that freedom of expression.

Like a robot, I went through the morning classes and at noon called Irene. She was quick to assure me Dianne was the same as when I had left her. She had gotten up late morning, eaten half a piece of toast, drunk a small glass of juice, read the newspaper, and after a short time gone back to bed. I was relieved to learn Dianne had eaten something. She had no appetite and I knew the pain was barely tolerable in spite of the pills she was taking.

I wanted to be home with Dianne. I knew Irene was taking good care of her, but I also knew I didn't like not being there. As soon as the bell rang signaling the end of my school day, I raced home. Mark and Irene were on the patio playing cards. I immediately asked Irene how Dianne was. She said the last time she had looked in on her, which was about a half hour before, she was dozing. That was good news because I knew she had not been sleeping soundly at night. I walked into the bedroom expecting to see Dianne

165

snoozing comfortably. Instead, her face was lined with pain, and as I bent to kiss her, I could see her forehead was damp with perspiration. She looked at me with pain and fear in her eyes. I asked her how long she had been having this pain.

"Not very long." Her voice was soft but firm.

"Where does it hurt?"

"My whole stomach area."

I lifted the sheet and looked at her stomach. The entire area was distended. I was dumbfounded. I had never seen anything like that before.

I felt a tightening throughout my whole body and a sense of panic set in. I knew when swelling like this happened quickly it was usually caused by internal pressure, but I couldn't imagine what kind of pressure could be causing this. Although Dr. Kempf had mentioned Dianne might have a tumor, he said nothing about this kind of thing happening.

So I said, "Gosh, honey, your whole stomach is swollen." She raised her head from the pillow attempting to look. The attempt was only momentary. She let her head fall back onto the pillow. I realized then for the first time that she didn't have enough strength to accomplish even this small task. The fact of her getting weaker every day never occurred to me. I knew she hadn't been eating as she usually had, but the significance of that lack of food just escaped me. I was focused on her strength and fortitude; I was focused on her getting relief from pain; I was focused on the approaching treatment; I was focused on knowing she was going to get better.

"How swollen is it?"

"Well, swollen enough so that it's pretty noticeable."

I ran my hand over her stomach and then I took her hand and did the same thing again. I knew I needed to do something.

"I'll be right back." I pulled the sheet back over her, ran my hand across her forehead, and kissed her lightly. I hurried to Irene and Mark still on the patio playing cards. Even though I wasn't angry with Irene, my first comments were accusatory.

"I thought you said she was sleeping. How long has it been since you looked in on her? She's in a lot of pain and her stomach is swollen. That couldn't have happened in just a few minutes."

Irene dropped her cards onto the table and getting up said, "Well, it hasn't been that long. She was sound asleep and I know it's not been more than an hour." By this time we were into the bedroom. Irene looked at Dianne's stomach and was as surprised as I had been. She felt Dianne's forehead and cheek and spoke softly to her. "I think we should call Dr. Kempf and tell him about this. We may have to take you to the hospital. Is that all right?"

Dianne nodded.

As we left the room, Irene said, "I don't understand that at all. Whatever this is must have happened quickly and recently. She was all right at noon. I went in to look at her and found her walking back to bed from the bathroom. I scolded her and told her I didn't want her up and walking around by herself and that she should call me when she needed to get up and I'd be right there. She just looked at me and said, 'Well, I needed to go to the bathroom.' I told her I didn't care what her mission was, she was to call me. She finally agreed. I looked in on her later and that was when she was sound asleep."

Irene said she was sure Dr. Kempf would hospitalize Dianne and the sooner I put in a call to him, the better off Dianne would be. I called the hospital and was told the doctor would be paged and he would call back. I waited 30 minutes and when the phone had not rung, I called the hospital again. This time I was more aggressive and was reassured again they were trying their best to find Dr. Kempf. During this time I was making repeated trips to the bedroom, checking on Dianne. Her pain had not decreased; if anything, it had gotten worse and the stomach area seemed to be more distended. I told her we had a call in to the doctor, and if she would just hang in there a few more minutes, I was sure she'd get some relief.

During all this, Mary arrived. She was just there if we needed anything to be done, she said. We apprised her of Dianne's condition, and she decided to hang around in case she could be of any help.

When 3 o'clock came and there was no phone call, I told Irene I could wait no longer. I couldn't bear seeing Dianne in such pain and nothing being done about it for her. None of us knew what was happening. Dianne was scared; I was worried and scared; Irene was worried but, outwardly, calm. I had to do something. So I did what my heart and my gut told me to do. I called the hospital again and told them I was bringing Dianne in. We would be there in thirty to forty-five minutes and would they please get that message to Dr. Kempf so he could see her as soon as she got there.

With that, I went into the bedroom and told Dianne I was taking her to the hospital. She asked if Dr. Kempf had called and I said "no" but the hospital staff would tell him she was coming so he'd be there when she arrived. I asked her if she thought she could walk to the car. She said she figured she'd give it a try. I eased her to a sitting position and swung her legs around to the side of the bed. I knew this change of position was extremely difficult for her. The pain was so intense I could almost hear it. Mary was on one side of Dianne and Irene on the other as I put Dianne's slippers on her. Mary and Irene half-lifted Dianne to her feet, and with their arms around her waist and hers around their necks, they started down the hall. Mark had gone outside to bring the car closer to the back door. I picked up Dianne's robe and started to follow them. They had only gone about six steps when Dianne stopped and said in a voice that was both surprised and exhausted, "I can't make it."

"You'll have to carry her," I said as I went around them.

Mary and Irene surrendered Dianne to my arms as they crossed their wrists and held hands to form a makeshift seat. They bent low to allow Dianne to easily sit and she put her arms around their necks. They carried her to the car that way. Mark had the passenger seat pushed way back and they carefully set her down. By this time she was perspiring profusely. It was not an excessively hot day, but Mark turned on the air conditioning. I climbed in the back seat behind Dianne and put my arms around her. I ran a soft damp cloth across her forehead hoping it would give her some relief and told her we were on our way to the hospital. I tried to assure her Dr. Kempf would see to it that the pain was taken care of and to try not to worry or be scared. She did not respond. She did not respond to anything I said or did throughout the forty minute drive. I silently prayed Dr. Kempf had gotten our message and would meet us at the hospital door.

I was functioning on a level that defies description. My mind was whirling; my body was taut as a bowstring; yet, from somewhere came the capacity to sound controlled. And all of this was surrounded by numbness.

Almost before Mark had stopped the car, I was in the lobby of the hospital. I quickly explained the situation to the attendant behind the desk and inquired as to the whereabouts of Dr. Kempf. After putting though a call to someone, he said Dr. Kempf was on his way. I asked him if he would please get a gurney so we could make Dianne more comfortable. He made another call. When no gurney appeared after five minutes, I asked him again. This time he left his post and disappeared. He returned in a few minutes with a wheelchair. He could not find a gurney, so he brought the next best thing. He took command as he pushed the chair though the hospital doors out to the car. He opened the car door, and speaking softly but firmly to Dianne, he said, "Just put your arms around my neck; I'll do the rest." She did as he requested. Then he picked her up and gently set her in the wheelchair. We followed him back to the information area where he stopped, put in another call, and turned to us and said, "Dr. Kempf will meet us on the second floor."

With the same care he previously demonstrated, the attendant transferred Dianne from the wheelchair to a gurney that had suddenly appeared. We all took the elevator to the second floor and then waited in the small room for Dr. Kempf to appear. He was there within minutes. He questioned Dianne as to the location and intensity of the pain, its onset, her activities, and what she had eaten. I asked him if there wasn't something he could give for some relief now, but he said it was necessary for her to have the pain so they could determine the problem. Without knowing where it was hurting and why, they could not make a diagnosis. Logically, I knew this made sense; emotionally, I disliked him for not being able to make Dianne more comfortable right THEN.

Dr. Kempf moved swiftly and with certainty. When he finished his cursory exam, he ordered tests on a "Stat" basis. Dianne was whisked away and we were left again to wait.

Almost an hour later Dr. Kempf reappeared. He told us Dianne had been taken to ICU and would probably be there for a couple of days. They would do further tests tomorrow and then he would consult with the other doctors on the possibility of surgery and/or therapy depending on the test results. He suspected Dianne's internal bleeding was related to her melanoma with either the liver or bowel. For now, she was in ICU and "resting comfortably."

"Can we see her?"

"Of course," replied Dr. Kempf.

Mark had chosen to wait in the car during all this, so Irene and I followed the doctor to the room where Dianne was. I looked at Dianne and she had none of the outward signs of distress as before and although tired, greeted us with half a smile. A tube had been placed through her nose and a reddish-brown liquid was being drawn through it, an IV was inserted in her right hand, and the usual machines were reporting their monitoring by flashing numbers. Even though this was an intensive care unit; even though she had been admitted in extreme pain; even though there was still much to be determined and dealt with, I knew she would overcome this minor setback and we would soon be home sitting on the patio again deciding the most propitious way to proceed. I knew we didn't have the luxury of several more years, but I did know we had at least one and a half. I leaned over and kissed her.

"Are you feeling any better?"

"A little."

"Well, Dr. Kempf says he's going to keep you here another day or so until he sees the results of the tests."

"Okay."

"Try to get some rest and I'll be back early in the morning. We'll do exactly as the doctor says and we'll have you back home in no time."

She nodded.

"I love you, sweetheart," I said. "And I'll see you in the morning."

"I love you, Ret."

We kissed.

My heart hurt as I glanced back at her lying there, knowing I had to leave her in this sterile surrounding all night. Then I thought about tomorrow when I would talk to Dr. Kempf, sure that he would tell me I could take Dianne home soon.

I would talk to Dr. Kempf all right, but that would not be his message.

Irene and I arrived at the hospital early the next morning and Dianne was awake and alert. Her stomach was still distended and painful. I was not happy with the level of pain she seemed to have, but I knew from talking to Dr. Kempf that until they knew the reasons for her discomfort any pain medication would mask the symptoms. She said Dr. Kempf had been in a couple of hours earlier and she expected to see him again early afternoon.

"How was your night?" I asked her.

"I didn't get much sleep," she said, irritated. "The woman over there moaned all night long. This is ridiculous."

I agreed and immediately found a nurse, repeated what Dianne had told me and asked if it was possible to move Dianne to another ICU room. The nurse assured me the woman was being moved out of the ICU within the hour. And she was. I was glad to see Dianne get a little angry. It was further proof to me that she was going to get better. It had been several days since I'd seen her react to an outside activity. I told her I had called Dick and that he was making arrangements to come down. I didn't know when yet, but he would call. We sat with her until they took her to x-ray.

That afternoon Dr. Kempf visited with Dianne. After determining she was alert and oriented, he discussed with her the findings of the CAT scan. Remembering we had agreed to have honest conversations, he told Dianne the cancer had invaded her liver which was the source of the bleeding. He wanted to keep her in ICU another day and if the bleeding persisted, they would plan to do an embolization. She still felt, as we all did, that the sooner something was done that would enable her to begin some form of therapy, the sooner she would be able to go home. I knew this summer would be severely different from any other summer, but it would still be our summer.

Dr. Kempf carefully explained the process of embolization. A long needle would be inserted up through the groin and into the liver where several arteries would be cauterized. Although it was painful and Dianne would undoubtedly experience considerable pain afterwards, it would be controlled by a morphine drip. Dr. Kempf asked Dianne if she understood what he had said and she nodded. We all had faith in Dr. Kempf; we trusted him completely and relied totally on his judgment. And so the procedure was scheduled for Friday.

By this time, the communications network was already underway. It wasn't long until our community of friends was aware of Dianne's condition, and the vigil began. Since Dianne was still in ICU, visitors were limited. The waiting room began to fill up and it stayed that way. Even in the early hours of the mornings, there would be women sitting close together speaking in the hushed tones that hospitals seem to dictate as proper. They speculated, reminisced, predicted, prayed, and loved.

Dianne expressed her desire to have no heroic therapy or resuscitation performed, but did want all the standard therapy including the possible embolization, chemotherapy, and/or surgery. Dr. Kempf questioned Dick and me about whether this thinking was consistent with her thinking of the past. We both indicated it was. At this moment I realized the importance of the Medical Consent forms Dianne and I had signed some time ago. Because now, as he asked the question, Dr. Kempf looked to Dick as her blood relative for primary validation. Dick nodded. Dr. Kempf then asked me the same question and I said it was. I knew then that if Dick had disagreed with Dianne's request for "no heroic measures," I could have overruled him. I had the consent form signed by Dianne which gave me ultimate decision-making power.

When I saw Dianne again that afternoon, we talked briefly about what Dr. Kempf had said. She had been given medication and so our conversation was intermittent. Dr. Kempf had been optimistic about the embolization procedure and so she was. And so I was. She was, as always, anxious to get on with it. She dreaded only the pain that would follow. I promised her it would be controlled. Her level of pain now was less and I was glad to see she was able to fall in and out of sleep.

On Thursday, June 7, Dianne was moved from ICU into a room of her own. Although she would look at me when I spoke to her, I felt our communication was becoming blocked. I would meet her eyes with mine and at different times saw understanding, pain, fear. I was certain that once this procedure was completed, our communication would be as it always had been.

After his morning visit with Dianne, Dr. Kempf asked Irene, Dick, and me to follow him to the conference room. Once there, he talked to us about prognosis, options, risks, and the critical status of Dianne. I had not heard the word "critical" used in connection with Dianne before and now when Dr. Kempf said it, it seemed a poor choice of word to describe Dianne's condition. In the loving manner I had come to expect and to appreciate, Dr. Kempf told us one option was chemotherapy. However, the usual chemotherapy response at best was a 20-30% reduction of the tumor with virtually zero chance of cure. If Dianne responded, then she could expect perhaps two to three months of useful life.

Another option would be to withdraw all care but he didn't feel this was indicated, nor did we. So if the procedure today was successful, he would begin chemotherapy in one to three days.

I sat on the edge of the sofa in the hospital's family room where this discussion had just taken place. I tried to concentrate on what Dr. Kempf had told us. I tried to think about what he had said and what it all meant. I needed to understand what had transpired this last hour. But the only words I could remember were "two to three months useful life." What the hell did "useful life" mean? And what month was three months from now? And what happened to the "eighteen months?" I needed to see Dianne.

I walked softly up to Dianne's bed, sat down, and took her hand in mine. She continued to have moderate blood loss and transfusions had been necessary. The tube that was initially inserted through her nose and into her stomach was still there sucking the bloody mixture into the disposal bag. Whenever she was thirsty, we gave her crushed ice, and no sooner had she chewed and swallowed it than it could be seen making its way out of her stomach through the tube mixed with the other dark liquid. I knew her throat was sore from the tube and that the relief she felt from the crushed ice was limited. But it was all I could do for her. That and swab her gums and teeth with the mint-flavored sponge on a small stick. I felt helpless. I felt inadequate. I felt deficient.

I felt hate. I hated seeing her like that. I hated her body for not responding. I hated the healthy women who came in to see her. I hated the nurses for continuing to draw blood from the hands that were already so bruised. I hated hearing the doctors refer to her as "the patient." I hated the machines surrounding her bed that seemed to be determining her fate. I loved her so much.

On Friday, June 8, the embolization was performed. After our long wait, Dr. Kempf informed us that it had been successful and the resulting pain, which would be considerable, would be controlled by a morphine drip. I was relieved to hear this.

Over the weekend the waiting room continued to be filled with our friends. They alternated between the waiting room and Dianne's room. With Dianne, they sat by her as she slept; they held her hand asleep or awake; they talked to her when her eyes were opened and it appeared she was listening; they talked to her when her eyes were closed and they didn't know if she was listening or not; they loved her from a distance; they loved her up close. Dianne drifted in and out of wakefulness. Her pain was obvious whenever the nurses would lift her or roll her onto her side. The slightest movement would cause her to moan—a sound I can still hear. During her periods of wakefulness, she wanted her mouth swabbed to assuage the soreness and crushed ice to relieve the dryness. The nursing staff continued to give her the gentlest treatment I had ever seen. They swabbed her mouth with mineral oil, bathed and massaged her using only the slightest movement, performed the routine blood tests with a loving touch, and always spoke to her with warmth and concern. Her pain seemed to be their pain.

Dr. Kempf predicted that, if Dianne's strength held up, chemotherapy could begin on Monday. If Dianne's strength held up? Dianne was one of the strongest women I had ever known. There were many days when she functioned on sheer determination alone. I had not a doubt that if the determining factors were Dianne's power and stamina, the road to recovery would begin.

On Monday, Dr. Kempf assessed Dianne's condition and determined to hold off the chemotherapy until she had gained more strength. Although she was awake, she was not asking or answering any questions and had become more non-communicative and non-responsive. Dr. Kempf told us she was scheduled for a scan and some other tests that day, and he would wait for those results before making any further suggestions.

I was aware of Dianne's lack of communication. I was also aware of her communication. I knew that every movement I made while I was in her room, she would follow with her eyes. She would watch my hand take hold of hers;

she would watch as I rearranged the blanket; she would follow my lips to hers. I *knew* that just because she wasn't saying anything did not mean she wasn't alert. What I *didn't* know was that the invader had silently found its way throughout Dianne's body.

On Tuesday, June 12, Dr. Kempf again called Dick, Irene, and me into a conference. Even though we had not had many of these "conferences," I dreaded them. I associated them with one more thing Dianne would have to go through before she could come home. Why couldn't they decide once and for all what to do, do it, and let Dianne and me get on with our lives?

Now, as before, inside the small room, Dr. Kempf spoke with the same caring tone as he discussed the latest test results. And, as always, he was honest. The scan revealed that the cancer had spread into Dianne's bone marrow and brain. He had consulted with other doctors on the case, and they agreed that any treatment could no longer be safely given. There was no reasonable chance of her condition improving. And he wanted to know, were we still in agreement with Dianne's wishes not to use any heroic measures to keep her alive, but to allow her to die with dignity? Suddenly all the sounds were muffled. In the distance I heard both Dick and Irene affirm this desire. I heard my own voice agree. Then I heard nothing. I tried to put what Dr. Kempf had just told us into some form I could understand: no more treatment, no chance of improvement, no heroics, die with dignity. Dianne was going to die. She was not coming home. We would not have the summer. She was going to die in this hospital right where she was.

"What kind of time are we talking about?" I think Irene asked that question.

Dr. Kempf didn't know. "It's difficult to say. A week, maybe. This cancer has spread with surprising speed."

A week, maybe? What was today, Tuesday? Did that mean Dianne would never see another Tuesday? My mind was speeding in its attempt to make some sense. My body shivered; I was cold.

We walked out of the conference room. I left Irene and Dick and went to see Dianne. She was sleeping. I sat by the bed, took her hand in mine, and just watched her. She didn't look like she was going to die. But she was. She opened her eyes and looked at me.

I could only say what I felt. "I love you, Dianne. I'm just crazy about you."

She looked at me with those wonderful blue eyes.

"Why don't you talk to me?"

After a long pause she said, "It – it's just so hard to think."

"Well, then don't. It's okay. I'll just talk to you for awhile."

And I did. I read some correspondence to her; I told her about the women who were there in the waiting room, but for one reason or another could not come in to see her; I talked about the dogs and the dichondra, about her garden and the algae starting to form in the pool; I told her she had stacks of mail at home all waiting to be opened by her; I told her I had a big brown envelope at home that was filled with notes and cards her students had written; I gave her a weather report. I didn't even know I was saying goodbye.

On Wednesday, June 13, Dianne went into a coma.

On Friday, June 15, at 6:45 PM, enveloped in love from the women who surrounded her, and while the sun was still warm, Dianne died. It was the last day of school.

CHAPTER THIRTEEN:

THE LESSONS OF GRIEF

My world ended. Not with a bang; not with a whimper; but with a deafening silence and jolting abruptness.

My world ended and nothing was the same. Not just externally where all around me everyone was doing as they had always done, totally unaware of the horrendous event that had just taken place, but internally as well. It hurt to swallow and I felt nauseous. There was a constant pain in my chest and I moved in a vacuum. My mind could not focus on any one subject for any length of time. Over the last few months people had given me books about death, dying, life after death, handling grief, how to survive a loss and various personal experiences that included all of those. Those books lay untouched. I was not interested in reading about anyone else's grief. I was not interested in reading anything. I was interested only in trying to make some sense out of what had happened, and come to grips with the reality that it really *had* happened.

I had lost my lover, my best friend, my anchor. No, I had not *lost* her. Lost is like misplaced or missing. When someone is lost, you search for them and, ultimately, you find them. I couldn't do that. Dianne was not lost; she was dead. I tried saying it aloud: "Dianne is dead." But my heart felt it was a lie.

And so I waited for the sound of her car in the driveway; I expected her to come walking down the hall; I looked for her in every room. At night I would lie on her side of the bed and hold her pillow. It smelled of shampoo and of the fragrance that was so uniquely Dianne. I could not believe I would never again lie beside her.

When I slept, the hours were few and fitful. My nights were simply hours of waiting for morning. In the dark I would go over and over the events of the last several months, trying to determine what we could have done that would have effected a different outcome. And I found no answer. And, incredibly, I thought of the days and years ahead without Dianne, refusing to believe they would ever come to pass. Surely, my heart told me, this was just a bad dream.

The days became weeks without my even knowing it. Time was no longer relative. It was just something that *was.*

Still unable to concentrate for any length of time, my head was filled with a myriad of thoughts and my mind raced from one to the other. I found no solace in any of them. These were the summer months Dianne and I were to spend together. The time we looked forward to, made plans for, and talked about all during the year. With the realization that I was alone came that god-awful ache that started in my throat and quickly coursed through every part of my body leaving only emptiness in its path.

During the weeks that followed, an array of friends stayed with me. A few, at different times, literally moved in for four or five weeks. Although I acknowledged and appreciated their presence, it was, at times, solid evidence that a change had taken place. Under ordinary circumstances, they would not be here.

Friends did their best in trying to fill my time. Invitations were issued for dinner, for overnight, for the weekend. But each one served only to make me more acutely aware of Dianne's absence.

The end of August arrived bringing with it the day I had scheduled to scatter Dianne's ashes. When Flo had picked them up in June, we made plans that on the first of September we would take them to "where the women were." And where the women were that weekend was at the West Coast Women's Music & Comedy Festival being held in the Santa Monica Mountains.

Flo, Coe, Dee & Susan were already at the festival and I drove up Saturday morning solely to fulfill the promise I had made to Dianne. Mid-morning, we walked among the trees and foliage bordering a dirt road Dianne and I had named "P" road. We had camped near this road at the last festival and it had served as our bathroom at night. As we walked, we each took a handful of ashes from the black tin box and gently placed them at the base of trees and shrubs feeling that in this way Dianne would somehow continue to contribute toward growth. I don't know what I had expected from this ritual. I guess I thought it would help make it possible for me to realize the finality, the irrevocability of death. And perhaps even find some comfort. This did not happen. I tenderly and tearfully scattered the ashes, but I could not relay that gray and white gravelly, semi-powdery substance to the dynamic, spirited person of Dianne. Cold and numb in the heat of the day, I drove home.

And then, suddenly, it was the opening day of school. I had no idea how I was going to manage that. I wanted to resign from life. I wanted to forfeit all my responsibilities. I wanted my life to be like it was. But I *knew* it never would be. I carefully admitted to myself I would have to find a vehicle that would make it possible for me to get up every morning, to function in the classroom and to get me through the unwanted days that stretched ahead. In the shadows of my thoughts, I recognized my need to keep in touch with reality. Following that was my awareness that I was still needed, albeit on a different and limited level.

I knew I had to water the dichondra and feed the dogs. These two responsibilities forced me to face each morning. The days at school became a blur. My body moved automatically, preprogrammed by a system that now seemed to be on "hold." I continued to wonder why I was in the classroom, engaged in a discussion on character development, when I wanted so desperately to be at home where the essence of Dianne was. And so, at each school day's end, I drove frantically to get home. And each day, as the garage door opened and her parking space was empty, I faced the awful truth again.

September ended.

October and November were mere repeats of September. Except everything became more intense: the pain, the loneliness, the darkness. I searched for a way to maintain a semblance of sanity. And found it. I found it in isolation.

I relegated myself to a sleeping bag on the floor of the family room. There, each day upon returning home from school, I would change into my pajamas, turn on the TV (which would run all night) and crawl into my sleeping bag. Rarely did I eat dinner. At 5:30 AM, I began again the ritual that had become my way of life: water the lawn, feed the dogs, drive to school, drive home, gather the mail, pet the dogs, get into my pajamas, turn on the TV and crawl into the sleeping bag --all the while begging for it all to go away.

One Sunday, as I lay in the sleeping bag in the early morning hours feeling certain all my remaining days would be like this, and knowing I no longer wanted to face them, I thought about taking my own life. It was just a few days after Dan White had committed suicide and the way he had done it seemed to be so easy: simply sit in the car in the garage, turn on the ignition, let the motor run, close my eyes and take an eternal nap. [Editor's note: Dan White was a former San Francisco City Supervisor who had killed SF Mayor George Moscone and gay Supervisor Harvey Milk in 1978]. I thought about it for several hours. Initially the prevalent feeling was exhaustion. I was tired: of making the effort, of the pain, of the emptiness. How wonderful to have it all go away.

In a moment of clarity I knew that if I pursued this line of thinking and feeling much further, I would certainly destroy myself. And I remembered how much Dianne had loved life, how disappointed she would be if I quit, how angry she would be if I didn't live out my life to the fullest. And I felt guilty even entertaining the idea of suicide. Did I really want to do that? Shivering with fear, I knew the answer was "no."

I needed to talk to someone. I called Jan. She listened as only a friend who cares will listen and she gave me firm directions that resulted in her monitoring my behavior for several hours. Ultimately my thoughts were unclouded even though my emotions remained the same.

The days dragged on. The nights were interminable. The weekends were nightmares. The holidays were a blur. Was this ever going to end? Would it ever get just a little easier?

One afternoon as I started to crawl into the sleeping bag, I realized nothing had improved. If anything, deterioration had taken place. I was losing myself. Having depended primarily upon Dianne for external validation of who I was, I now seemed incapable of re-establishing an ego. I was directionless, rootless. Instinctively at that moment I knew that if I didn't change the course of my actions now, it would soon be too late.

Three days later I started what was to be almost a year of therapy.

During that time, I came to terms with Dianne's death, at least enough to be able to begin the long, slow journey to recovery. I realized that I related differently to the world, just as it did to me. I began to think of myself as a whole caring individual, unique unto myself with a special identity. I was not just the surviving half of a couple, I was a total person by myself. I became comfortable with tears and understood there was no special place reserved for crying. Avenues of reintegration into the world appeared and I began to focus on living. I gathered strength from the pain of missing Dianne; I found hope in the memory of her dreams. I began to gather the pieces of my life ready to begin again.

It took me two years to write the first draft of this book. It was one of the hardest tasks I've ever attempted. It was also one of the most therapeutic and rewarding.

Before I began I was certain that, 37 years later, I would be able to easily write in detail about my years in the Air Force and the events leading to my Undesirable Discharge. It came as a surprise that in remembering and reliving those years, I still felt a great deal of anger, resentment, and hurt. I expect some residue will always remain.

I included my time in the service, not only because it was an important episode in my life, but because I believe society needs to be informed about the treachery and betrayal its government is capable of in its treatment of homosexuals. And the havoc an Undesirable Discharge wreaks on a life forever.

There remains one incident related to my discharge that is still unresolved. In 1954, while visiting Irene in Sacramento, I attempted to call Marie—my off-base lover who I had been forced inadvertently to "out." I had long wanted to talk with her, to try to make her understand why I did what I did. And so I called her sister in an effort to find Marie. Her sister told me in cold, flat tones that Marie wanted nothing to do with me. She told me that two men from the OSI had come to their house, asked questions of her mother and dad, quizzed Marie and other family members about our relationship and had left the family in a state of confusion, fear and anger. Marie, especially, felt she had been deceived, used, and abandoned. I could not believe what I was hearing. The men of the OSI had promised me they would not contact Marie, that they did not need her statements, that they had no interest in her. To all the other lies they had told me, they added another one.

More than ever then, I wanted to see Marie and explain the circumstances. But that was not to be. She refused to speak to me. Over the years, I tried to contact her. I never did. Finally, I stopped trying. It is the one thing in my life I regret. The picture of Marie and her family being confronted by the OSI remains lodged in my imagination, accompanied by my feelings of frustration and disgust.

But somehow patriotism is still deeply ingrained within me. Kate Smith's singing "God Bless America" still stirs my soul and I'll *always* love a parade!

Sharing Dianne's illness and death was unimaginably painful. There were days when I could write only a portion of a page. But I knew it had to be done. I had learned so much and I needed to share this knowledge. I desperately wanted to let people, lesbians in particular, know that not only loneliness and pain inevitably follow the death of a lover, but that behavior is considerably altered.

Scenes and situations that were familiar and comforting became strange and tense. Being with other couples was constant proof that Dianne had died. Feelings of envy and resentment surfaced. I found myself hating my coupled friends.

My inability to reach out, to ask for help, to express a need, was crippling. I had never before had any problems asking for what I needed from anyone: Dianne, friends or family. Now I seemed incapable of making the overture. I waited for friends to call, to make the first move. I didn't understand that what was at the core of this different behavior was the fear that I might be rejected. My ego was not strong enough to withstand this possibility and rather than take the risk, I chose not to ask for anything.

I recognized that the world saw me differently. Dianne and I had always been able to comfortably socialize with any number of women, single or coupled. Now, no longer coupled, I was a threat to these very women.

It became impossible to make a commitment more than one day in advance and sometimes that was too much. I tried to commit to future dinner invitations and at the last moment was not able to meet that commitment. At times I would follow through on an invitation and at some point later I would leave with an abrupt goodbye.

Consequently, my behavior became bizarre. I know it was discussed among my friends. This seemed to be totally unexpected and no one understood. I couldn't help them understand because I didn't understand. I only knew that I was barely functioning and their chastising sent me reeling. It would have been so much easier had they given me the latitude to be indecisive and inconsistent, undependable and ungiving, without making me pay a price.

I was restless. It didn't matter where I was. No place was where I wanted to be. Peace of mind eluded me.

I was short-tempered and disinterested in others. I had neither the time nor the inclination to hear about anyone else's life.

I know now some things my friends could have done or not done, said or not said, that would have assuaged my pain and comforted me.

My need to talk about Dianne was immediate and desperate. It was important that the people who knew her spoke to me of her. I needed to reminisce about her and have others share with me their experiences. I told everyone of my need, individually and in groups, but only a miniscule few heard my plea. I waited for someone to mention her name in any context: "I thought about Dianne today," "I wish Dianne were here to see this," "Wouldn't Dianne have loved this concert?"

But I waited in vain. It did not happen. It was suddenly as if she had never existed. Months later when I asked why, their replies were invariably the same: "I didn't want to make you feel bad." DIDN'T WANT TO MAKE ME FEEL BAD? I FELT bad! Talking about Dianne was not going to make me feel worse; just the opposite; it would have been comforting.

From those who were anxious for me to get beyond my grief came the god-awful opinion that "in time you'll forget." What a dreadful thing to say! I didn't WANT to forget. I NEVER wanted to forget how Dianne smelled and tasted, how her body felt against mine when we danced or made love, how her pillow always smelled of "White Shoulders." Forget? Never.

Some, in their search for something to say to me, reached into their religious beliefs: "God works in mysterious ways" or "God must have needed her more than we do." I could not agree with, or even listen to, those words. I acknowledged their need to say that, but it was not my need to hear it. For those who share the same religious beliefs, this may answer the questions and ease the pain, but for me there was no comfort in hearing that some nebulous creature they believed all-powerful needed Dianne more than I did.

Others, submerged in their own pain, could find nothing to say to me and so avoided me. This, the sin of omission, is perhaps the greatest. Unable (or unwilling) to analyze their actions, I was hurt and angered. For the survivor, the answer is so simple: a hug, an "I loved her, too" or "I'll miss her" is sufficient. There is no need to be poetic or verbose. The love comes through.

Everyone gave advice, most often in the form of a "should." "You really should dispose of her things now." I couldn't. I just couldn't. In the recesses of my mind I knew that when I was ready to remove her "things" I would. Didn't they understand that for now they were all I had? "You should stop living in the past, Ret." The past was all I had. There was no looking forward to a happy future. There was no looking forward, period. If I stopped living in the past, I stopped living. I wish someone had told them that. "You should go out more, socialize and meet new people." I had no energy to socialize and no enthusiasm to meet new people." I was totally depleted. I needed them to support my efforts, insignificant as they may have seemed. I needed them to visit me, if only for a few minutes.

Now, as I finish writing this, six years after Dianne died, I am learning well the lessons of time. I realize there is no uniform process for grief and grieving. It has its own timetable and it differs with each individual. However long it took me to cope with Dianne's death, to establish a new life, and to regain a sense of self-worth would be determined by me. And there are truths I know now: I know that a certain void will always be there; I know there will always be some degree of pain and sadness; I know that I will always miss her. I know that her life had more of an impact on me than her death, and that bitter or sweet, the memories become more precious as the years move on. I know, too, it's possible to love again, and that that love has nothing to do with my love for Dianne except that I am aware of its value because I have experienced how quickly it can be taken away.

EPILOGUE:

THE COSTS OF SILENCING

by Jon Pahl

Loretta Coller began writing her *Memoirs* for a specific purpose—to deal with the grief of losing her life partner. After she had written them, however, she began to see how her life story had other implications that might be useful to readers. Consequently, she began to seek a publisher for them, just about the time her life was cut short. Before narrating the events that led to her death, though, I first want to highlight in this Epilogue a bit more about Loretta's career as an educator.[30] She was, after all, an American teacher, and her commitment to her career can perhaps prepare us to see how even her death might communicate a lesson well worth learning.

Loretta taught for twenty years. According to a profile in the Winter, 1982 Sunny Hills High School *Excalibur*, a publication produced by the school's journalism classes, Loretta began her teaching career at Lowell High School in Whittier in 1967.[31] She taught English there for five years. In 1972, she volunteered to teach in a special program for young people who were hospitalized in the psychiatric ward at the La Habra Community Hospital. As Loretta recalled, the kids in the ward were "homicidal, suicidal, delinquents, and runaways."

Loretta's class at the hospital started with three students, three hours per day. The class grew to an even dozen. After a year, Loretta suggested to the Fullerton School Board that  the hospital program become fulltime. They agreed, and appointed Loretta the only instructor. Loretta was responsible for teaching math, science, reading, history, art—you name it. "It was like a one-room country school," Loretta remembered. Among its benefits, she continued, was that "my vocabulary expanded. I heard words I hadn't heard in years!" Loretta ran the program for five years, until its demands wore her down. "It was emotionally draining, but I'm glad I did it," she stated. Two students graduated from the program—one from high school, one from 8th grade.

After her hospital stint ended in 1977, Loretta was transferred to Sunny Hills High School near Fullerton, where she remained for the remainder of her career. She taught English for one year, then revived the school's defunct drama program. Each year thereafter, she cast and directed two plays. In fact, she also chose the scripts, designed and helped build the sets (often with Dianne), selected the costumes, ordered and sold the tickets, and arranged for the printing of the programs.

I have several of those programs in my possession now, courtesy of Loretta's sister Bette. They give glimpses of her impact in the lives of young people. Cast members often signed them with tributes to Loretta. "Thanks for being the greatest teacher I've ever had," wrote a young man with a minor role in *South Pacific*. "Drama opened up a whole new wonderful world to me," wrote another, a cast member from

Oklahoma! And one student summarized Loretta's significance in her life by writing: "Thank you, thank you, thank you for all your support, compassion, dedication, and wisdom. I love you." Little wonder, given such relationships, that Loretta could simply assert: "I love to teach." What motivated her, she added, was the modest, and obviously fulfilled, desire to "make a difference in a life or two."

Throughout her career, Loretta earned a reputation for being a no-nonsense teacher with a compassionate heart who enjoyed life. The *Excalibur* profile reported, for instance, that some students found her intimidating, until they got to know her. She sometimes yelled, and "got a little excited." And she often rode a motorcycle to and from school, but regretted being "unable to do wheelies coming up the hill." The profile also highlighted her feminist activism, including her support for the National Organization for Women, the ill-fated Equal Rights Amendment, and various pro-choice and human rights groups.

The profile treated with respect Loretta's "lifestyle." "Coller never had any intention of getting married," the interviewer put it. "I wanted to be free," it quoted Loretta as saying. The student author couldn't resist a little editorializing: "Her life style is not for everybody." But the last words in the profile were Loretta's own, and they echo the first lines of these *Memoirs*, with a typical dash of humor: "If I had to do it over again, I wouldn't change a thing. I grew up to be a happy adult. . . attractive, voluptuous, sensuous, and rich," Loretta said, undoubtedly with a hearty laugh. She was an American teacher.

She was also "deeply closeted." What she remembered in her *Memoirs* from her teaching career was her fear of being "outed," and the pain of having to keep silent about her lifestyle. She wanted people, notably the parents of her students who hugged her after a successful play, to know that she was a lesbian. She wanted them to know "as a statement from all of us." But throughout her career, she felt "this was practically impossible." She felt compelled to keep silent.

And this silencing may have killed her. On June 2, 1994—barely six months after Loretta had told me she'd written her *Memoirs*, my father called me with the news. Loretta had been critically wounded by a gunshot the night before. "She might be paralyzed," my dad said. I was stunned. At the time, all that anyone in Wisconsin knew was that Loretta's assailant was a former lover, Janet Greene (the "Scarlett" to whom her *Memoirs* were dedicated), and that another woman, Martha Pereida—had also been injured.

As that phone conversation continued, I didn't recall ever having met Janet, although I knew that she and Loretta had lived together for some years. I'd met Marty in January during our Rose Bowl visit, and liked her. My parents, however, knew Janet quite well. Most memorable to them was a trip she and Loretta had made to Wisconsin in 1989, when Loretta came out in dramatic fashion at her fortieth high school reunion. I remembered vaguely that Loretta had said she'd "broken up" with Janet shortly before our January visit to California for the Rose Bowl festivities. "Loretta told me she felt smothered," my Mom added.

According to newspaper accounts, Janet Greene had met Loretta Coller in 1969, when the two taught together briefly at Lowell High School.[32] Janet had apparently been physically attracted to Loretta from that first acquaintance. Like Loretta and Dianne, Janet was active in the Southern California Women for Understanding. But out of respect for Loretta's partnership with Dianne, Janet chose not to pursue her attraction. Even when Janet joined Loretta on the faculty at Sunny Hills High School, in 1982, she kept her distance, although she was friendly with both Loretta and Dianne, and the women had mutual friends.

After Dianne's death, Janet joined the many women who served as caretakers for Loretta. These women cooked meals, cleaned house, and generally helped keep Loretta coherent enough to work. From time to time Janet would spend the night, sometimes for days on end. That wasn't unusual. Many of Loretta's friends did the same thing, including my Aunt Dorothy Martin. But Janet apparently had more than altruistic motives. "Janet saw it as her mission to help Ret get through [her grief]," a mutual friend commented. By 1986, her mission became a romance, and her overnight stays at Loretta's house became extended stays.

The two did share much in common. After 1982, they taught together at Sunny Hills. Janet, like Loretta, was well respected there. Her peers named her Teacher of the Year in

1988. Both women enjoyed sports, camping, and the outdoors. And both had been active in SCWU. In 1987, in conjunction with her retirement from teaching, Loretta sold the house she'd shared with Dianne. She then purchased a home in Glendora, and invited Janet to move in with her. By the time Loretta penned the last draft of her *Memoirs*, probably in late 1993, Janet was one of three women— along with Billie and Dianne, to whom they were dedicated. Janet's nickname of "Scarlett" gives a fascinating clue to the character of their relationship. Many of Loretta's friends called her "Ret." Loretta was also tall and strong, and given her love of drama, it did not take too much imagination to see her in the role of Rhett Butler—the hero of the romantic epic *Gone with the Wind*. Janet—who was wiry and petite, thereby became "Scarlett."

The two played their roles with panache in a party Loretta threw to celebrate Janet's 50th birthday on May 22, 1993. "Well, Fiddle dee dee, impossible as it may seem, Scarlett will be Fifty on May 22," read the invitation Loretta wrote for the "Gone with the Wind Costume Party." Guests were asked to "dress to reflect the Civil War era," and not to bring gifts. They were promised a "Mint Julep Social" beginning at 4PM, with a buffet at 6:00. On the cover of the invitation, in sepia brown tones, was a picture of Loretta and Janet in their own costumes for the evening. Ret dressed as a nineteenth-century southern gentleman. Janet wore a flowing hoop skirt and picture hat.

If the couple shared many interests, then, including a playful side, they also had very different personalities. Already at the time of the Gone With the Wind party, things had begun to fall apart between them. One of the issues was retirement planning. In 1988, they had purchased land together in a small Oregon town. Janet harbored dreams of retiring there. Loretta enjoyed camping at the site, but enjoyed her time with other friends in Southern California, and her spacious poolside home, too much to leave that venue permanently.

Other strains developed. Janet was generally a private and even shy person. Loretta liked to party. As a newspaper report summarized it, Loretta "drove convertibles. She collected 50s memorabilia, had a jukebox full of 45s. She bought guns—mostly rifles—because she loved the gun-slinging romance of the Old West. She once tap-danced "Happy Birthday" at a friend's party. In a G-string. Topless."[33] Initially, when Loretta retired and began working as a disc jockey for private parties, Janet would accompany her, sitting in a corner, knitting. Over time, Loretta became more involved in these events. She bought her own equipment, and began trying out some of the stories in these *Memoirs* as stand-up comedy. As Loretta became more vocally out, Janet backed away. Eventually, she just stopped attending Loretta's gigs.

Finally, in September, 1993, Loretta decided to end the relationship. Janet tried desperately to hang on. A neighbor of Loretta's friends recalled, in the aftermath of the breakup, that "Janet moved in and out a couple of times. She wanted to get back together, but Loretta didn't want her back."

Loretta, perhaps naively, kept in touch with her estranged lover. This naturally fueled Janet's hopes. "Loretta felt very, very responsible for Janet's well-being," one companion of Loretta commented. "She didn't want to see Janet hurt. She was trying to alleviate Janet's pain and anxiety."

But Janet's behavior turned increasingly erratic. She began to lose weight, chain-smoke, and drink heavily. Already in July, 1993, when the couple was still living together, she threatened Loretta with a gun. Then one night in May, 1994, after Loretta had evicted her, Janet crawled back into the house through a pet door, and again threatened her former partner with death. On both occasions, Loretta calmed Janet down. Despite warnings from her friends, though, Loretta refused to out Janet to the police. During daylight hours, and when Janet hadn't been drinking, the two got along quite well. Loretta from time to time would visit Janet at Sunny Hills. And Janet looked forward to occasional dinners with Loretta at area restaurants.

It was around this time, in May, 1994, that my father had his last contact with Loretta. Actually, the contact came via a letter that she sent to Donald Goers, another graduate of Shawano High School, class of 1949. My father—in fact my family generally, including me-- was the object of its humor. In it, Loretta explained why she would be unable to attend the 45th class reunion. It is such a typical piece of exaggerated humor that it deserves quoting in full.

"Hi Don," the letter begins:

I am unable to attend the reunion this year because I cannot leave the state. This is because I am being sued by my neighbors and the City of Glendora. Apparently the December/January visit of the Fred Pahl family (Barb, Jon, and Andy) to attend the Rose Parade and Bowl game got completely out of hand. The first charge was "disturbing the peace" (later changed to "inciting a riot.") A second charge of "displaying to excess" colors that had suggestive overtones [the Badgers' colors are red and white] was filed naming Fred as primary defendant, with Barb as an accomplice. A third charge of "vagrancy and bogus bargaining" was filed naming the two sons as primary offenders. Apparently, they spent numerous hours sitting on curbs, approaching strangers and attempting to scalp their Rose Bowl tickets.

Please do not make this public knowledge. Fred and I have been friends since 1945 and I don't want any static. So as they say in the James Bond movies, this is "for your eyes only."

I believe I'll save myself (an exercise in futility!) for the 50th Reunion.

Regards to anyone who cares------

What had happened as we sat on the curb, of course, was hardly "vagrancy." It was there that Loretta had told me she'd written her *Memoirs*. She would never make the 50th Reunion.

Meanwhile, as May passed and Janet continued to pine for Loretta, her colleagues at Sunny Hills watched with alarm as Janet became increasingly unstable. Loretta had tried to move on. She began a relationship with Martha Pereida—who had been friends of Loretta and Dianne since 1980. Some of Loretta's friends continued to urge her to go to the police. One said: "It was like a speeding train coming at you. We all could see this. Ret, in her naïveté, never believed that Janet would do her harm. I told her to remove the guns from the house. I told her to take Janet's hysterics seriously. I suggested a restraining order, but she didn't want to expose or hurt Janet."

And around 7:30 PM on the night of June 1, while Loretta and Pereida were having dinner in Loretta's Glendora home, Janet Greene crept into the house through an unlocked patio door. She took a gun from Loretta's nightstand in her bedroom, and surprised Loretta and Marty with it. She ordered them to sit down on a nearby couch.

Greene then fired a warning shot into the piece of furniture. "This is the way I wanted to find the two of you," Pereida recalled Greene saying. "First I'm going to kill Marty so you can see her die." Pereida then lunged at Greene, according to police reports. As the two women wrestled for control of the gun, and as Loretta moved toward them to intervene, the gun discharged three times. The first shot hit the ceiling. The second shattered Pereida's leg. And the third tore into Loretta Coller's chest, where the bullet lodged in her spine. Greene's blood alcohol level at the time was .14—well over the legal limit.[34] And it was that single bullet that ended Loretta Coller's life. She died on June 18, 1994, after seventeen days in the hospital. She was sixty-two years old.

Greene pled innocent, and claimed that the shooting was an "accident." She also intimated, without any evidence, that her relationship with Loretta had been abusive. She did express remorse over the killing almost immediately after it happened, and her friends raised the funds for her defense. She was found guilty by a jury of second-degree murder and assault with a deadly weapon, and sentenced to eighteen years to life in prison. At the time of her sentencing, the judge instructed Greene that "you are a lucky woman. With the evidence produced in this trial, you should have been found guilty of first degree murder."

Janet Greene died in jail in November, 2005. She had suffered for years from Lupus—a disease that had begun to impact her already in the early 1990s. In jail, she attended Mass, and was regular at AA meetings. I was never able to arrange an interview with her. The last I heard from Marty Pereida was in July of 1994, when she wrote a long letter thanking my parents for their support of her. She was planning at the time to return to work, but still suffered serious side effects from the gunshot wound to her leg.

Loretta, of course, was simply gone. Shortly after her death, friends and former students came together to mourn her passing, and to offer testimony about Loretta's meaning in their lives. The memorial service was held at Northwest College on July 10, 1994.[35] About 150 were in attendance. The service lasted three hours. Janet Doyle, a leader in the SCWU, planned the service, and credited Loretta with being "an inspiration to many of us. . . . She dealt with coming out in the '50s, a tough time." Doyle also recalled Loretta's undesirable discharge by the Air Force during the McCarthy era, but then reported that Loretta had petitioned to receive an upgrade in discharge—and won.

Other speakers offered the kinds of accolades students had given Loretta throughout her career. Former student Linda Sypien recalled how when she could not afford to pay to commute to study drama at UCLA, Loretta handed her a gas card and told her to "use it as much as you need to." When Sypien offered to pay Loretta back, Coller simply said: "When you find someone you believe in, you do the same." Kevin Hoban, a 1981 graduate of Sunny Hills, claimed that Loretta "taught me without ever having to say it—the acceptance of people. It starts by accepting yourself." And friend Margie Mullen summed up the feelings of many: "My sorrow is not just about Ret. My sorrow is she's gone from this world." The bulletin from the service, printed on lavender paper, had a picture of Loretta on the front, a couple of poems in the middle, and the words "She Did It Her Way. . ." on the back.

Now, death was the inevitable end, one way or another, of the life-story of Loretta Coller—as it is the end for every living being. The legacy of Loretta's life, however, remains to be made by those who carry on after her—by people who knew her intimately, and by people who have come to know her—as in many ways I did, through the pages of her *Memoirs*.

Some readers might be tempted to impose on Loretta's story a melodramatic or moralistic plot.[36] It would be easy enough to construct heroes and villains out of this tale, and to divide the world through Loretta's story into simple dichotomies of good versus evil, righteous versus unrighteous. Loretta surely could be a hero-victim to other lesbians. And her murder lends itself quite obviously to the construction of a villain.

But melodrama reduces complex human beings to stereotypes. Loretta began writing her *Memoirs* precisely to get *out* of a self-imposed victim's isolation. Her dedication of them to Janet suggests that she would never want one of her partners to be seen as simply a villain. And she shared enough of her struggles and flaws to make it abundantly clear that she did not want to be seen as a hero. Her life, in short, was the same rich and irreducible blend of desires and actions, fears and fascinations, failures and successes that constitute the contingencies of human living for anyone, anywhere, and anytime.

Loretta's death, similarly, cannot easily lend itself to moralistic judgment. Some might exploit the scandal of her murder to condemn "the homosexual lifestyle." After all, there has been in the early twenty-first century a concerted effort underway to organize political consent in the United States over and against gays and lesbians, and to construct a society in which the silence that Loretta suffered for so many years again becomes an imposed, or tacit, norm.

Surely such moralism is unwarranted. Domestic violence, which is the most apt way to describe the circumstances under which Loretta died, is hardly a uniquely gay or lesbian problem. And heterosexuals like me can by no means claim to have it all figured out when it comes to building a quality life together with another person.

If there is a moral lesson to be learned from the life and death of Loretta Coller, then, I would hope it would be to deepen compassion for the struggles of people living in same-sex relationships, and to strengthen commitment to creating a more just and open society. I also suspect, however, that to discern the deepest and final lessons to be learned from Loretta's life, we must move beyond matters of individual moral judgment, and into the realms of politics and spirituality.

Politically, as I've repeated like a mantra throughout, Loretta was an American teacher. I chose this title for at least two reasons. First, it suggests that we need to recognize and honor the contributions to society of educators like Loretta, and support the educational institutions that so often struggle for funds in the richest nation on the earth. Second, it suggests that we can learn from Loretta's life ways to redress some of the systemic violence in American culture that inhibits fulfillment for so many.

All Loretta asked through her narrative is for the freedom to live with the same kind of private intimacy and public legitimacy that heterosexual males like me can take for granted. When politicians, authorities, and the laws of the land stigmatize and segregate gays and lesbians, and when citizens go along, we impoverish our society.

And when we silence gays and lesbians, we put their lives at risk. Isolation, real or imagined, can escalate desire. And desire repressed can explode into violence. Is it any wonder, then, that people like Loretta often don't see police, the criminal justice system, or other authorities as advocates in cases of conflict? Recall Loretta's experiences with authorities, first through the Church, and then through the State. Now put yourself in her shoes. Even if Loretta had called the police on Janet Greene, how could she have had any confidence that the police would have been able to intervene sensitively and effectively?

So there is a powerful political lesson to be learned from the life and death of Loretta Coller. We are stronger when we build a society that includes people out of human compassion, rather than one that excludes people out of fear or prejudice. And we will build such a society through the contributions across generational lines of teachers like Loretta.

Finally, though, I think the meaning of Loretta's life is spiritual. Loretta lived a life of love and laughter. One of my favorite quotes comes from the 14th century English mystic,

Julian of Norwich. I share it often with my students. Julian was a nun who established convents and worked with victims of the plague. She knew evil. And she concluded: "The way to fight evil isn't to cudgel the brain (or as I translate for modern students—'to bang your head against a wall.') The way to fight evil is to live a life of love, and laughter."

Ironically, then, I see Loretta Coller—for all of her ambivalence about the Catholic Church in which she was raised, as a lot like a nun. Like many nuns, she was a teacher. And like many nuns, she loved drama, whose roots of course lie in the realm of ritual. Loretta was what historians of religion like me call a spiritual "seeker." She was a restless soul.

And yet, she found meaning and purpose in staging and performing dramas. I suppose at one level, then, we could call her life a tragedy. Tragedy, Aristotle suggested, was about catharsis. We identify with the flaws of the protagonist, and learn from the protagonist's fate, in order to purify ourselves of similar flaws, and steel ourselves for our own inevitable struggles with suffering and death.

Loretta had her flaws. She was not always completely honest. She mistrusted even legitimate authority. She was a little naïve. And she liked guns, one of which eventually killed her. Her life was, on one level, an American tragedy.

Loretta could appreciate tragedies. But she loved musicals. Often, musicals get dismissed by high-brow critics. Tragedy is serious. Catharsis is important. Musicals are superficial.

I'm convinced this judgment is itself superficial. Music is perhaps the only universal language. It can be listened to with pleasure across cultures and centuries. It connects us to experiences of beauty, awe, and joy. And who is to say that beauty, awe, and joy are any less vital to life than purity?

Loretta Coller loved music. Her *Memoirs* practically ring. She couldn't carry a tune, but she tried her best to stay in the choir of her Catholic school, anyway. She couldn't keep a pitch, but she sang in the shower at the top of her lungs. She directed *South Pacific* and *Oklahoma*! And she worked as a disc jockey.

So, perhaps the most fitting way to wrap up the story of Loretta Coller's life is to say that her life was, like any human life when one looks for the beauty of its plaintive longing, a song. The song of the life of Loretta Coller was the song of an American teacher. It was sung in the cracks between the black and white keys. It was a unique and fragile melody, a little bit funny, yet rich with harmonies of authentic and irreplaceable beauty. Loretta's song—whose lingering refrain sings through the prose of her *Memoirs,* can elevate any of our lives. I didn't know her well. I know her better now. And I wish she was still around for me to express how I've come to love her, and how I've learned from her. Most of all, I wish she was here to see her life-story in print. I hope she'd be proud. And I know she'd throw a party. There would be music. And we'd laugh.

INDEX OF PHOTOS

ENDNOTES TO INTRODUCTION
AND EPILOGUE

[1] See here Chesire Calhoun, *Feminism, the Family, and the Politics of the Closet: Lesbianism and Gay Displacement* (Oxford University Press, 2000).

[2] Mary Ann Humphrey, *My Country, My Right to Serve: Experiences of Gay Men and Women in the Military, World War II to the Present* (NY: Harper Collins, 1990), pp. 10-17.

[3] Among the instigators of the trend is Howard Zinn, *A People's History of the United States* (Houghton-Mifflin, 1980). Best known, perhaps, is the work of the late Stephen E. Ambrose, *Citizen Soldiers: The U.S. Army from the Normandy Beaches to the Bulge to the Surrender of Germany, June 7, 1944-May 7, 1945* (Simon and Schuster, 1997).

[4] See, for instance, Melissa Etheridge, with Laura Morton, *The Truth Is: My Life in Love and Music* (Random House Trade, 2002), and Betty DeGeneres, *Love, Ellen: A Mother/Daughter Journey* (Perennial Currents, 2000). Both of these works have merit, but reflect a later generation than Loretta's memoirs, and obviously are shaped in light of the subjects' celebrity. Closer to Coller's generation is the memoir from Lillian Faderman, *Naked in the Promised Land* (Boston: Houghton-Mifflin, 2003). Faderman is without doubt the foremost scholar of lesbian history, and as her title suggests, writes in a self-consciously revelatory, if not exhibitionist style (she once worked as a burlesque queen) that Coller did not embrace.

[5] See, for example, the interesting lesbian memoirs by Louise A. Blum, *You're Not from Around Here, Are You: A Lesbian in Small-Town America* (University of Wisconsin Press, 2001); Jan Clausen, *Apples and Oranges: My Journey to Sexual Identity* (Houghton-Mifflin, 1999); and Claudia Bepko, *The Heart's Progress: A Lesbian Memoir* (Penguin USA, 1997). Bepko shares Coller's Catholic upbringing, but brings a

professional agenda to her writing, as a practicing psychotherapist, that Coller did not share.

[6] See on this process, the fascinating interpretation of Chris Glaser, *Coming Out as Sacrament* (Westminster/John Knox, 1998). For a sampling, see Stephan Likosky, ed., *Coming Out: An Anthology of International Gay and Lesbian Writings* (Pantheon, 1992). More general, but invaluable, is the *Encyclopedia of Lesbian and Gay Histories and Cultures*. 2 vols. (Garland, 1999).

[7] See on this theme Margot Canaday, "Building a Straight State: Sexuality and Social Citizenship under the 1944 G.I. Bill." *Journal of American History* 90, no. 3 (2003): 935-57

[8] My efforts to contact Loretta's confidantes in the organization were unsuccessful, but a percentage of any profits from this project will be donated to establish a Loretta Coller Scholarship Fund.

[9]The matter of lesbian identity is discussed by Rosa Ainley, *What is She Like?: Lesbian Identities from the 1950s to the 1990s* (Cassell, 1995).

[10] See, for instance, the manifold books that encourage gays and lesbians to "repair" their desires, notably Richard Cohen and Laura Schlesinger, *Coming out Straight: Understanding and Healing Homosexuality* (Oakhill Press, 2001). Suffice it to say that I think these books are driven by a moralistic ideology and bad science in ways that are damaging to both civil society and individual lives. For a longer history, see Byrne F. S. Fone, *Homophobia: A History* (Henry Holt, 2000). For a more detailed accounting of violence against gays and lesbians, see *Crimes of Hate, Conspiracy of Silence: Torture and Ill-Treatment Based on Sexual Identity* (Amnesty International USA, 2001).

[11] Often, people who are afraid of gays and lesbians mistakenly associate homosexuality with pedophilia. In fact, the vast majority of pedophiles are heterosexual, and every objective study has documented that there is no greater tendency toward pedophilia in the homosexual community than among heterosexuals. Furthermore, gays and lesbians who are teachers do not recruit from among the young, or try to defend their sexuality in the classroom. Most teachers who have been lesbian or gay have, rather obviously, been deeply closeted—hardly an effective recruiting platform. And those who have come out publicly have the same boundaries on sexual relations with students as do any other teachers. See "Facts about Homosexuality and Child Molestation," University of California, Davis, at http://psychology.ucdavis.edu/rainbow/html/facts_molestation.html, as cited 12/30/2008.

[12] See, for instance, Ryan D. Johnson, "Homosexuality: Nature or Nurture," at http://allpsych.com/journal/homosexuality.html, as cited 12/30/2008.

[13] "I think it's an innate thing," she says, in the Humphrey essay. See "Loretta "Ret" Coller," in Mary Ann Humphrey, p. 10.

[14] See on the complex origins of identity formation and politics surrounding lesbians, Ellen Lewin, ed., *Inventing Lesbian Cultures in America* (Boston: Beacon Press, 1996), and especially Lewin's "Introduction," pp. 1-11. I have also found very helpful Janet R. Jakobsen and Ann Pellegrini, *Love the Sin: Sexual Regulation and the Limits of Religious Tolerance* (NY: NYU Press, 2003), who contend that "sexual freedom is a form of religious freedom," protected by the First Amendment. By grounding gender identity in sexual *practice*, and recognizing such practice as protected by the "free exercise" clause of the First Amendment, Jakobsen and Pellegrini render the nature-nurture dichotomy irrelevant. As they put it, gay sex "does good, is good," in and of itself, regardless of its biological or cultural origins. It is only when gay sex is perceived as a problem that its regulation becomes necessary.

[15] In her essay in the Humphrey collection Coller is, again, more open about her desires. In her typical style, she writes that "I never entered the military with the idea of finding other lesbians," but when "I got into basic, I thought I had been transferred to hog heaven! No damn kidding. Lordy!," p. 11.

[16] On the medical origins of the label "homosexual," see Jennifer Terry, *An American Obsession: Science, Medicine, and Homosexuality in Modern Society* (The University of Chicago Press, 1999).

[17] For a broad overview of the history of lesbianism, see the classic by Lillian Faderman, *Surpassing the Love of Men: Romantic Friendship and Love Between Women from the Renaissance to the Present* (Perennial, 1998[1981]). See also Faderman's history of lesbians in the modern U.S., *Odd Girls and Twilight Lovers: A History of Lesbian Life in Twentieth-Century America* (Columbia University Press, 1991), and her evocative *To Believe in Women: What Lesbians Have Done for America—A History* (Houghton-Mifflin, 1999).

[18] The standard critical edition is *The Autobiography of Benjamin Franklin*, ed. Leonard W. Labaree (Yale University Press, 2003).

[19] See here my *Youth Ministry in Modern America: 1930-the present* (Hendrickson, 1999), which traces what I call the "long liminality" or transition to adulthood among American youth in the last half of the twentieth-century.

[20] This contrasts somewhat with the classical picture of the history of coming-of-age as depicted by John Modell, *Into One's Own: From Youth to Adulthood in the United States, 1920-1975* (University of California Press, 1989).

[21] Loretta's life-story thus reinforces what psychologist Carol Gilligan, and many other writers, have suggested about distinctive paths to women's maturity. See most notably Carol Gilligan, *In a Different Voice: Psychological Theory and Women's Development* (Harvard University Press, 1993).

[22] Increasingly, historians are seeking to discover the histories of children and youth, and frequently historians are frustrated by the lack of access to narratives of children's experiences. Often, the only things we know about children in history are the things adults who ran youth-serving institutions have said about them. As a result, children generally appear to be either angels or demons, innocent or damned, pure potential or perpetual problems. Of course, Loretta's childhood memories were recorded late in her life. And while they are therefore subject to the rust of memory that is nostalgia, they also do not reveal any overt institutional agenda, and were not written in light of preserving some achieved public status or reputation. In fact, the interplay between allegiances in Loretta's narrative makes it a fascinating primary source revealing the difficulty of access to "children's" history. I happen to be an active member of an academic guild to study such questions, namely the Society for the History of Childhood and Youth (SHCY), which was founded in 2001. You can visit the Society's webpage at http://www.h-net.org/~child/SHCY/, as cited 6/26/2006.

[23] See here Robert Orsi, *Between Heaven and Earth: Religious Worlds People Make and the Scholars Who Study Them* (Princeton University Press, 2005), and especially Chapter Three, "Material Children: Making God's Presence Real for Catholic Boys and Girls and for the Adults in Relation to Them," pp. 73-110.

[24] The history of Catholicism in the U.S. is succinctly told in Jay P. Dolan, *The American Catholic Experience: A History from Colonial Times to the Present* (Doubleday, 1985). Dolan directly contends that early twentieth-century Catholicism in America "was clearly a religion of authority, and people learned not only to pray, but also to obey. Being

Catholic meant to submit to the authority of God as mediated through the church—its Pope, bishops, and pastors. In such a culture, the rights of the individual conscience were deemphasized, as each person was conditioned to submit to the external authority of the church," p. 224. Loretta lived with this structure throughout her life, even as she left the church. For the "plus" side of the Catholic-schooling ledger, see Anthony S. Bryk, Valerie E. Lee, and Peter B. Holland, *Catholic Schools and the Comon Good* (Harvard University Press, 1993). It is the rare individual who can both come out and stay in the church. Among them, as an articulate advocate, at least for gay men, is James Alison, *Faith Beyond Resentment: Fragments Catholic and Gay* (Crossroad, 2001).

[25]See, for example, the groundbreaking work of Alice Kessler-Harris, *Out to Work: A History of Wage-Earning Women in the United States* (Oxford University Press, 1982). For a more recent guide to gender history, see *A Companion to Gender History*, ed. Teresa A. Meade and Merry E. Wiesner-Hanks. (Blackwell, 2004). Three recent monographs on women at work in twentieth-century America include Nan Enstad, *Ladies of Labor, Girls of Adventure: Working Women, Popular Culture, and Labor Politics at the Turn of the Twentieth Century* (Columbia University Press, 1999), Francesca Sawaya, *Modern Women, Modern Work: Domesticity, Professionalism, and American Writing, 1890-1950* (University of Pennsylvania Press, 2004), and Margaret May Chinn, *Sewing Women: Immigrants and the New York City Garment Industry* (Columbia University Press, 2005).

[26] Along with Humphrey, see Ellen Schrecker, *Many Are the Crimes: McCarthyism in America* (Princeton University Press, 1998). On gays and lesbians in the U.S. military, see Allan Berube, *Coming Out Under Fire: The History of Gay Men and Women in World War Two.* (Free Press, 1990) and Randy Shilts, *Conduct Unbecoming: Gays and Lesbians in the U.S. Military* (World, 1997). Both Berube and Shilts attend primarily to the stories of gay men, and Shilts only briefly touches on the McCarthy era. The most comprehensive work on the general attack on gays and lesbians during the McCarthy-era is David K. Johnson, *The Lavender Scare: The Cold War Persecution of Gays and Lesbians in the Federal Government* (University of Chicago Press, 2004).

[27]In the Humphrey essay, the depth of this trauma is evident, even after she has secured her upgraded discharge (to "General," in 1979). She writes: "To this day, I have such a negative attitude toward the government and the military that it's hard for me to discuss it without becoming emotionally upset. . . . When I got my upgrade, I didn't feel like I had *gotten them*, because after they've *had you* for forty years, it's

hard to feel like you you've *gotten them*. I pay my taxes because I don't want to go to jail, but I'd never do anything service-oriented for this country, and I'm not a patriot. You know, I figure that I gave them all I had so very long ago and they just fucked me over. So fuck them now! I would hope that what I gave after the military proves the value of my contributions as a lesbian. I still see absolutely no reason for that regulation that discriminates against people like me," pp. 17-18.

[28] Loretta's experience in this community reinforces the arguments of John D'Emilio, *Sexual Politics, Sexual Communities: The Making of a Homosexual Minority in the* United States, 1940-1970, 2nd ed (The University of Chicago Press, 1998[1983]). Local histories of gays and lesbians are beginning to emerge. See, for example, Susan Stryker and Jim Van Buskirk, *Gay by the Bay: A History of Queer Culture in the San Francisco Bay Area* (Chronicle Books, 1996) and George Chauncey, *Gay New York: Gender, Urban Culture, and the Making of the Gay Male World, 1890-1940* (Basic Books, 1994).

[29] I have a book forthcoming, tentatively entitled *Blessed Brutalities: The Religious Origins of American Violence*, that documents the long history of violence as a religious process in the formation of the American nation.

[30]Loretta clearly saw her teaching as her primary contribution to society. In her essay in the collection by Mary Ann Humphrey, *My Country, My Right to Serve: Experiences of Gay Men and Women in the Military, World War II to the Present* (NY: HarperCollins, 1990), she imagined speaking to the parents of the children she taught, who would (she was convinced) have been scandalized by her sexual orientation, and she writes: "I'd like to say to parents, "God, do you realize that this woman, this teacher, this drama coach, who has made all the difference in your child's life, is a lesbian? . . . I'm sorry you couldn't have really known me all of those years. . . . Then perhaps, just perhaps, you would have thought differently about gay people in general. But I can tell you this, that I loved teaching your children, and like it or not, I was a positive influence in their lives!" Now, doesn't that say something about lesbians?," p. 18.

[31] Beth Meberg, "Portrait: Loretta Coller," *Sunny Hills High School Excalibur* 13(Winter, 1982): 10-13. This publication, and other materials cited in this Epilogue, will be preserved along with my papers and the original manuscript of the *Memoirs* in the archives of The Lutheran Theological Seminary at Philadelphia, Philadelphia, Pennsylvania.

[32] A series of articles in *The Orange County Register (OCR)* documented the couple's relationship and Coller's death, funeral, and Greene's trial, and I depend on them throughout the following pages. See most notably Ricky Young, "O.C. Teacher Charged in Shooting," *OCR*, June 5, 1994, Metro Section, p. B1; Jessica Crosby, "Teacher Recalled for Legacy of Kindness," *OCR*, July 11, 1994, Metro Section, p. B1; Mike Gordon and Jessica Crosby, "What Pushed Her Over the Edge? Lost Love Turned the Teacher of the Year into a Killer," *OCR,* August 1, 1994, News, p. a01. The articles are available on-line, at http://www.ocregister.com/, as cited 12/30/2008.

[33] See Mike Gordon and Jessica Crosby, "What Pushed Her Over the Edge? Lost Love Turned the Teacher of the Year into a Killer," *OCR,* August 1, 1994, News, p. a01, online at http://www.ocregister.com/

[34]The details are recorded in an article by Anne C. Mulkern, October 12, 1995, at http://www.ocregister.com, Article ID OCR639456.

[35] See Jessica Crosby, "Teacher Recalled for Legacy of Kindness," July 11, 1994, at http://www.ocregister.com, Article ID OCR556099.

[36]These possibilities are drawn in part from the fascinating historical work by Lisa Duggan, writing about an earlier era but a similar episode of domestic violence. See *Sapphic Slashers: Sex, Violence, and American Modernity* (Durham, NC: Duke University Press, 2000).

CPSIA information can be obtained
at www.ICGtesting.com
Printed in the USA
FFHW010811150319
49534586-56436FF